Contents

Contributors

Kate Fennell works as an Assistant Producer on documentaries with the independent production company, Liberty Films. She was raised in Conamara and Galway and currently lives in Dublin. She graduated from Trinity College, Dublin, with an honours degree in Russian and Classical Civilisation. She has travelled widely and has always got itchy feet! She worked for two and a half years in St Petersburg and Istanbul. She speaks Russian, French and German fluently.

Anna Heusaff was born in Dublin and raised through the medium of Irish. She is of Breton and Irish stock. She spent seventeen years working with RTÉ, as researcher, reporter and producer/director of a range of programmes. Since 2002, she has been working freelance on various television and writing projects.

Lorcán Mac Gabhann was born and raised in Stillorgan, on the southside of Dublin, and has spent all his adult life working in the Irish-language sector with groups such as Conradh na Gaeilge and Foras na Gaeilge. He is currently employed as Head of Glór na nGael. Voluntary positions include Chairperson of Foras Pátrúnachta na Scoileanna LánGhaeilge, Treasurer of Gaelscoileanna, and Chairperson/Founder of Gaelscoil Thaobh na Coille. He is father to three children, Clíona (12), Ciarán (10) and Séadhna (8). The views that are detailed here are his personal views and do not necessarily represent the views of any of the above organisations.

Ciarán Mac Murchaidh lectures in the Department of Irish at St Patrick's College, Dublin City University. He has published articles and essays in *Irisleabhar Mhá Nuad*, *Léachtaí Cholm Cille* and *An tUltach*. He is the author of *Cruinnscríobh na Gaeilge* (Cois Life, 2002; 2nd edn, 2004) and is interested mainly in eighteenth-century Irish religious literature and the teaching of grammar.

Neasa Ní Chinnéide is from the Corca Dhuibhne Gaeltacht. Educated at University College, Galway, and the University of Wisconsin-Madison, she has a background in geography and archaeology. She became a television presenter and later a producer in RTÉ, working mainly in current affairs, and later as Department Head. She was a member of the founding Authority of TG4, Chair of the Celtic and Television Festival and Vice-Chair of the EBU (European Broadcasting Union) documentary group. She is currently working freelance and at the time of writing is Chair of the Irish Committee of EBLUL (European Bureau for Lesser Used Languages).

Muireann Ní Mhóráin is a founder member of Comhluadar, the support organisation for Irish-speaking families, and was its first chairperson (1993-2002). Along with her husband, Gearóid Ó Conchubhair, she is raising three children through Irish in Dublin. Formerly a teacher and a post-primary school inspector, Muireann is currently the Chief Executive of An Chomhairle um Oideachas Gaeltachta agus Gaelscolaíochta. She wrote the essay in this collection wearing her 'cap' as a parent.

Éilís Ní Dhuibhne was born in Dublin. Among her recent published works are *The Inland Ice* (Dufour, 1997) and *Cailíní Beaga Ghleann na mBláth* (Cois Life, 2003). She writes children's books under the pseudonym Elizabeth O'Hara. She has won the Stewart, Bisto and Butler Prizes for her work. Her novel *The Dancers Dancing* (Review, 1999) was shortlisted for the Orange

Prize for Fiction in 2000. She is a member of Aosdána and works part-time as an archivist in the National Library.

Máirín Nic Eoin lectures in the Department of Irish at St Patrick's College, Dublin City University. Her publications on various aspects of Irish language, literature and culture include *B'Ait Leo Bean: Gnéithe den Idé-eolaíocht Inscne i dTraidisiún Liteartha na Gaeilge* (An Clóchomhar, 1998). Her latest book, a study of literary responses to cultural displacement, *'Trén bhFearann Breac': An Díláithriú Cultúir agus Nualitríocht na Gaeilge* will be published by Cois Life in 2004.

Breandán Ó Doibhlin was born in Tyrone and received his secondary education in St Columb's College, Derry, and his university education in Maynooth, in Rome and at the Sorbonne. He is Professor Emeritus of Modern Languages at the National University of Ireland, Maynooth, and has been Rector of the Irish College in Paris since 1984. He was chief translator and editor of the Irish-language version of the Catechism of the Catholic Church (*Caiticiosma na hEaglaise Caitlicí*, Veritas, 2001). A novelist, playwright and critic, he founded the Maynooth school of criticism in the 1960s. He is the author of many works of scholarship, criticism and translation including *Néal Maidine agus Tine Oíche*, *An Branar gan Cur* and *Iníon Mhaor an Uachta*.

Donncha Ó hÉallaithe hails from Clonmel originally. Living in the Cois Fharraige Gaeltacht for the last thirty years, he has been involved with the Conamara-based Gaeltacht Civil Rights Movement and Comharchumann Chois Fharraige; the pirate television experiment, Teilifís na Gaeltachta, out of which grew An Feachtas Náisiúnta Teilifíse, the campaign for a separate Irish-language television channel; and the setting up of the annual community arts festival Pléaráca Chonamara. A maths teacher in the Galway-Mayo Institute of Technology, he has produced a detailed analysis of the data from the 1996 census on the use of the Irish language, which provided a measure of the extent to which Irish was used in the various Gaeltacht areas.

Lillis Ó Laoire lectures in Irish language and literature in the Department of Languages and Cultural Studies at the University of Limerick. He is also Director of Ionad na nAmhrán, a project researching traditional song at the Irish World Music Centre, UL. His study *Ar Chreag i Lár na Farraige: Amhráin agus Amhránaithe i dToraigh* was published by Cló Iar-Chonnachta in 2002. An English-language study of song on Tory Island is expected from Scarecrow Press in 2004.

Pádraig Ó Mianáin was born in Dublin to an Irish-speaking family, raised in the Donegal Gaeltacht and has been living in Portstewart in County Derry for nearly fifteen years. A PhD graduate in Irish Studies from the University of Ulster, he is currently Senior Editor of An tÁisaonad Lán-Ghaeilge, an Irish-language educational publishing company in Belfast. He is very active in Gaelic games, and a keen musician. Pádraig is married to Susan, an Irish teacher, and they have one daughter, Cliodhna, who is one year old.

Gabriel Rosenstock is a poet, haikuist and translator. He is also a member of Aosdána and the author/translator of over one hundred books. Recent titles include the travelogue *Ólann Mo Mhiúil as an nGainséis* (My Mule Drinks from the Ganges) (Cló Iar-Chonnachta, 2003) and the coffee-table book with American master photographer, Ron Rosenstock, *Hymn to the Earth*.

Alan Titley is the author of novels, stories, plays and literary scholarship. His work has been translated into several languages including Italian, German, Croatian, Albanian, Romanian and even English. He has won many literary prizes including The Pater Prize for International Drama (Australia), The Stewart Parker Award (BBC), and the Butler Prize of the Irish-American Cultural Institute. He is Head of the Department of Irish at St Patrick's College, Dublin City University.

Editor's Preface

'Who needs Irish?' is a phrase that one often hears in Ireland. It was chosen as a title for this book because it almost always provokes a response. Irish is the storehouse of so much of our heritage, our traditions, our literature, our spirituality, and our lived experience as a people and as a nation that it should come as no surprise that it can produce such strong reactions. But if the language is capable of arousing such emotions as anger, apathy, or sympathy, then surely it is important for us to be as fully informed as possible abut the issues involved – regardless of what stand we might ultimately take on the matter. Why is there such a range of feelings surrounding the Irish-language question? Why does the debate come across as being so polarised? How does one avoid becoming stereotyped in the debate? *Who Needs Irish?* tries to answer some of these questions.

Issues to do with language are never simple. We use it every day and think nothing of it, and yet language touches the very soul of our being. Language is the vessel used to communicate everything from the desire for food, to declarations of love, to the formation of complex thought. When cultural and political ingredients which have affected the course of Irish affairs are added to the mixing-bowl of language, we end up with a potent dough. Add to this the fact that the contact that many people in Ireland have had with the Irish language has been one of unpleasant coercion, and we end up with a serious challenge indeed.

It is important to point out that there are currently two debates taking place regarding the Irish language – one which is ongoing in the Irish-language media and one which takes place sporadically in the English-language media. Quite naturally, perhaps, the debate in the Irish language appears to be more multi-dimensional than the debate in English, but, of course, it is limited to that body of people who, because they know the language, can easily follow it. At the same time, the discussion in English is critically important to the welfare of the Irish language because it is the medium through which everyone is able to follow the arguments. This debate, however, could be so much richer were more people to become involved in it and were more people to realise the extent to which the debate reaches into other areas of concern outside the purely linguistic. 'Who Needs Irish?' is an attempt to enrich the discussion in English by introducing into it the multi-layered approach of the debate taking place in Irish.

A wide range of contributors has been invited to reflect on the language, including parents, language activists, writers, poets, academics and those working in the media. They are people who have made definite personal choices about the role they wish Irish to play in their lives and I am extremely grateful to all of the essayists who took the time and trouble to become involved in this venture. There is something for everyone in this book of essays. It is this editor's hope that you, the reader, will enjoy these contributions and, more importantly, find them informative with regard to the myriad issues which are involved in the Irish-language question. Come to this book with an open mind and allow the voices speak to your heart as well as your head. Even lovers of the language do not always agree about what is best for it, but one thing that cannot be questioned is the belief that all these writers share: that there is an intrinsic worth in preserving the Irish language for ourselves, for our children and for the generations still to come – and that is the greatest challenge of all.

Ciarán Mac Murchaidh
February 2004

Acknowledgements

I would like to take this opportunity to thank a few people who have made my task as editor a great deal easier than it otherwise might have been. I wish to thank Dr Máirín Nic Eoin whose endless energy and enthusiasm is a constant source of encouragement to me. Dr Liam Mac Mathúna, Registrar at St Patrick's College, was very generous with his time and advice and extremely supportive of the venture. I frequently had good reason to be grateful for the guiding hand of Toner Quinn in Veritas Publications and I wish to record an enormous debt of gratitude to him here. Finally, I wish to thank my wife, Karen, who stands patiently by as I get caught up in various projects and is always there when I come out the other side.

How Did We Get Here From There?

Alan Titley

My grandmother's speech was peppered with words I had never heard before. She spoke about putting a *sceach* in the *bearna*, or getting water from the *tobar*. There was a place across the field known as the *carraig*, with that soft 'g' which had not yet been Englishified. There were neighbours who were 'Horrigans', who would now have their names spelt and pronounced as the more conventional 'Horgans', with an 'r' which is quickly being unroughed. My mother to the end of her life spoke of the calves of the leg as 'collops' (*colpaí*). They came from a place only about ten miles from Cork city. I later learned from the 1911 census that my grandfather had entered himself and his eldest children as native Irish-speakers, and this was no place in which the message of the Gaelic League had penetrated. The no-landholders with the use of one field and no beasts were not ripe for any message of cultural nationalism. With a shock, I learned that he must have been telling the truth.

I give this as an illustration of that past which very few of us know. We reach out our hands and we touch an Irish-speaking realm not all that long ago. Irish-breathing Ireland is never more than a few generations away. No matter what part of the country we come from there is a secret history of which nobody spoke. It was a history of shame, of self-deprecation and of self-denial. It was also a history of just getting on with life in the new dispensation, as it always is. The present and the future smothered the past, but the past came back to revisit us. A goodly deal of Irish life is inhered in this struggle between remembering and forgetting.

We are all beholden to the ghosts of yesteryear. We are plonked into the here and now with the suppositions of the past moving through us while we float on the suppositions of the present. The nineteenth century was a time of great forgetting. If we can fatuously speak of the Irish people as a collectivity, and it is always dangerous to do so, then we can hazard that they wished to put the past behind them and bury it with not much ceremony under a new Anglicised dispensation. The pressure to do so was extraordinary.

The Irish language had drained from the great institutions and had stagnated in the unstirred and unstirring pools of the poor. Their church had made a devilish bargain with the state that provided it didn't support sedition it would eventually be given tolerance and even respectability. Their politicians looked to London for favours much as ours do to Brussels. A state within the great British state, a seat at the table, a strong church, a slice of the civil action, some land reforms; these seemed to be the modest aims of the people. The deal was never spelled out in any document, or plan of campaign, or political treatise, but it seemed as palpable as the breathing day. Ireland would Anglicise in tongue, Catholicise in religion, and respectabilise in society. This is, in effect, what happened.

No Irish political leader of any standing in the Irish Parliamentary Party cared a spud for any cultural programme. Charles Stuart Parnell, for all the passion he aroused in the populace and elsewhere, did not see 'Irish culture' – in any of its manifold or centrifugal scattered meanings – as having a part to play in his march of a nation. Politics was a determinedly secular craft, in the sense that it had no business in meddling with the soul of a society. Even such 'romantic' language would have been as incomprehensible to him as it can be embarrassing today. All that tosh and guff was outside the loop of land reform and business and commerce and the 'real' world of management.

But for all that, life doesn't move and shake in just the way the managers want it. Within a few short years of Parnell's death a cultural sea-change had turned the country around. The story of what we call the Irish Renaissance has been told and examined and pored over many times. Wherever its precise ripples began it culminated in a cultural explosion which is conventionally accepted to include the Anglo-Irish Literary Renaissance, the founding of the GAA, and the growth of renewed interest in the Irish language. Lady Gregory described it as 'all that stir and thought' which led to the establishment of the Irish Free State. Historians may argue about the details of the influence of that broad movement, but few would disagree that it played a vital and envitalling part in the independence struggle. As a consequence, it left its precise mark on the nature of the new Irish state.

Daniel Corkery said that this was the first time in history that a nation state was institutionally backing the Irish language, and that this was going to be its saving instrument. He was a firm believer in the doctrine that what one state had pulled asunder another could put together again. And for all the faults of the state and the education system over the following generation, most people who can speak and read Irish today do so as a direct consequence of state policy.

Thinking back on it, the attempt to 'revive' the Irish language was the most radical and revolutionary policy that the state set out to do. There are many things which that state can be proud of: its initial housing programme, its building of hospitals instead of prisons (until recently), its peaceful non-alignment in the mad butchery of the twentieth century; but these are things that you expect civil society to engage with. But having a cultural policy which attempted to recreate a new society and reverse the attrition of years was something quite unique.

My parents only encountered Irish in their final years in primary school. For most of their schooling the curriculum was indistinguishable from what was being provided in Fetherstonehaugh or Fife. They retained a few words with a kind of dogged pride, and my mother could give a garbled rendering of 'An Maidrín Rua'. If my maternal grandparents were probably native Irish-speakers within an evening echo of Cork, my father's mother came from a more documented Irish-speaking area in East Cork. My parents, then, were cast into that gap between the abandoned language and its new rebirth in the schools. Those people a few years younger than them were taught Irish from their first day in school.

The generation who went to school in the 1920s and 1930s learned Irish with a fervour that did not exist before or since. There is very little evidence that this was done in any way reluctantly. Both anecdotal and biographical records seem to assert a pride and an engagement with a brand new world. There was a general acceptance that Irish was the future, so that crass materialism and national self-belief came together in an alliance that is normally unlikely.

Teachers flocked to the Gaeltacht and were 'retrained' in a curriculum that was wholly different to that designed for the 'happy English child'. Preparatory colleges were established in order to give native Irish-speaking pupils a positive discriminatory leg-up into teaching. In most societies teaching is that profession which first gives the rural poor their initial step on the ladder into middle-class respectability. In most societies teaching is that profession which is loved from below and disdained from above. For Irish-speaking Ireland and for people from the neglected westlands whose English was still scoured, clumsied and uglified by their recent association with Irish, it proved an uplifting boon. Although it might be stretching things to say that Irish was 'sexy', it was certainly fashionable, and those that didn't think so kept their emasculated vowels in proper silence.

Revolutions, however, run out of puff. Rhetoric grows tired and ideals do not match reality. The great talk of a new dawn dribbled back to a wet-grey afternoon in an everlasting Toomevara. Nobody ever said so, but the idea that if you taught everybody Irish, and taught it well, then everybody would eventually go on to speak it, seemed increasingly remote. There was an undistributed middle between the logic of teaching and the conclusion of talking. While national schools did their best, the secondary system was more tepid, and third level turned the other cheek. Children did leave the primary school with a good grasp of Irish, but this was often dissipated when they entered a more so-called 'vocational' secondary system, and vanished like snot off a shovel when the real world of the university or the tech called the shots.

The first word I learned at school was *'doras'*. A lovely nun, who I learned later must have been an extra in *The Sound of Music*, said to the packed ranks of corduroyed boyos that this was a new word, and that when we went home we should say, 'I am going to close the *"doras"'*, rather than the door. If I believed in symbols I would say that it was an opening into a new world for me. Later that year, I was sent to deliver a message to the head nun and was told what Irish words I should utter. I practised them down all those hundreds of miles of polished corridors and arrived at the Principal's office of shiny brass and sin-stained wood. As soon as she answered the door, and peered out at me through her plastic square and holy eyes, the words scrambled in my throat. I did say something, but it was probably more like Sanskrit than Irish. She rapped back at me in Urdu, and I retreated through the wilderness with my tears.

Later, the geometrical grammar of the *tuiseal ginideach* clogged up my sense as if on hemlock I had choked, but I can still quote the first pages of *Neidín* and *Jimín Mháire Thaidhg* off by heart. My hands were singed because the plural of the Irish noun is as unregulated as the free market. I bear the scars of *Gramméar Gaeilge na mBráithre Críostaí* and am none the wiser. I sat beside a boy who was nicknamed 'Browl' because he couldn't get his tongue and lips around that delicately shaped *breall*. But I never heard any of my mates bad-mouthing the language, certainly no more than any other subject which was often approached with a leather in one hand and a leather in the other. But neither do I think that any one of them thought it would be 'revived' in that wholehearted coast-to-coast sense which somebody like Douglas Hyde envisaged. At least we never discussed it in the yard while sucking fags behind the oil-tank. We were aware that Irish was important to us as people, and to the country as a civic society; but a design, or even a strategic plan as they say now, plotting or directing a revival never rose up in our heads.

That was because there never was one. There were good and serious and positive actions, mainly in education. Broadcasting did a lot to show that the language lived beyond the chalk. A scholar looking for Irish in a rough area of Kerry, which is just about anywhere, was told: 'Ah, there was never any Irish here until the radio came.' There was a lot of genuine tokenism in public life, but as we now know to our cost, that genuine tokenism was far better than the thin-lipped silence of today.

Because the state always spoke of the 'revival' as being the aim of the teaching of the language, when that aim was patently not going to materialise, a certain despondency often laced with cynicism began to take root. People began to ask 'Why?' A realistic promotion of bilingualism doesn't have the ringing call to action that the clarion of revival had. And culture doesn't butter any mangles. And individual fulfilment and personal development and literary insight and the wonders of creation began to be abandoned throughout the education system in favour of the economic tooth and claw at just about the same time as Irish was being laid quietly but firmly aside. To say that Irish was 'a refreshing breeze for the wearied and disgusted heart of the modern world' as one scholar did at the turn of the twentieth century; or that it was 'unpolluted with the very names of monstrosities of sins which are among the commonplaces of life in English-speaking countries' as another did at around the same time would be laughed out of the court of public opinion fifty years later. One generation's idealism becomes another generation's butt of derision.

Some of this arose from a selective depiction of what an Irish-speaking community might be. Any brief examination of Irish-language discourse will immediately reveal that the most lively and acrimonious debates took place within it. It was as varied and as pluralistic a place as can be imagined. Patrick Pearse – once revered as a secular saint but now depicted as a sweaty terrorist – urged Irish writers to look to Maeterlinck, Ibsen, Tolstoi, Gorki, Jokai and to study the literatures of the world. He was an outward-looking international cosmopolitan. Pádraig de Brún translated *The Odyssey* and *The Divine Comedy* into Irish. There were nativists, of course, who sought to build a new society out of an imagined folkworld, but the elevation of rural Ireland into an icon was not confined to Irish-speakers. Nonetheless, Irish-speakers and their attendant culture were often cruelly parodied as being backward, loutish, hayseedish, dogpussed and joyless. An example of this is Sean O'Faolain's editorial in his brass *Bell* in 1944, where he lampoons the lovers of the language as 'perfervid Gaelic addicts', who are against 'all modernisations and innovations,' 'inbred in thought', 'utterly narrow in outlook', who live in a 'delightfully befuddled condition' of a 'fairy-tale fantasy' endeavouring to promote a 'Gaelic master-type'. Anyone can pluck mischief from billions of words and millions of utterances, and O'Faolain was as good at his propaganda as he was at throwing his mother down the stairs.

This kind of full-frontal assault was the Panzer division of more sneaky sniping. It is difficult to say precisely when the ideal of the Irish language in state policy topped the hill and began to slide down the other side. Probably shortly after the great war between Fascism and Communism. There were certainly no new initiatives to promote the language in the

1950s. From the 1960s on it was a fairly rapid retreat, certainly in education. The number of Irish-medium primary schools declined from 420 to 160 between 1961 and 1979. Secondary education suffered similarly just at that vital time when free secondary schooling for all became a reality. An organisation to remove Irish as an essential subject in the Leaving Certificate and for positions in the civil service was largely successful. Small 'unviable' Gaeltacht schools were closed, rupturing delicate societies. The preparatory colleges which ensured a steady supply of fluent Irish-speakers into the teaching profession were discontinued. The Government unbelievably refused to request that Irish be made an official language of the European Economic Community when we joined up. The standard of Irish required for members of An Garda Síochána was lowered. It looks like a litany of dismantling, and it is.

There is some unrich irony in the fact that the earlier generations schooled well in the language grew more crusty and cynical than more recent generations who know it less well. Speaking Irish on a street in Dublin I was asked by a native 'What language is that?' There is further irony in the fact that such a conversation might have happened more frequently in the six counties of Northern Ireland, but is hardly likely to today. There are always honourable exceptions, but it is difficult to trawl to mind many politicians who see support for the language as a central part of their mission. The private sector who have all the 'readies' would hardly see sponsorship of some kind of language attempt as moving off near the bottom of their lists.

Some of this is undoubtedly cyclical. The rapid abandonment of the language in the nineteenth century was replaced by the great rediscovery of the revival, which in turn has been replaced by a *laissez-faire*, live-and-let-live or not, as the case may be, lazy tolerance which drifts with the tide and blows in the wind. But that rapid abandonment of the nineteenth century was preceded by three centuries of attrition. The final act of language change is always the result of a long series of blows and thumps and softenings-up. We got it in the neck so long that the words fell out of our throats. We presumed that the job of getting them back in would be quite easy.

I remember when I was in secondary school wandering the streets of Cork city gathering signatures for what was known as the 'Let the Language Live' campaign. It was an attempt to get popular support on the eve of the publication of a government white paper on language policy. Knocking on doors is never a pleasant job, whether it be selling raffle tickets or looking for signatures. I was met with courtesy and sympathy and a positive attitude. These were people of good will. A few years later I stood on the back of a lorry outside a church after mass while canvassing for the independent Gaeltacht candidate in West Galway. It was a *breac-Ghaeltacht* area in north Conamara, where *breac-Ghaeltacht* usually means that Irish has been abandoned by the younger generation and is being hailed farewell with little regret by the older. I still see the hostility in the eyes of the people as I rallied my enthusiasm and held forth with what I thought was a kind of eloquence. It was not a political hostility, but a hostility to the fact that somebody might do a positive thing for the language that they were just dumping. These contrasts illuminated the paradox of the language. Many of those who have it, either as native speakers or those who have learned it with much credit and toil, don't shed a tear as it falls away. And those who don't have it at all feel the need to call it back.

There is a reason for this. We have never resolved our identity crisis after the retreat of the language. The greatest part of Irish intellectual discussion is given over to who we are, and why we are as we are or whether we are at all; and are we a post-colonial society, and where do we stand now, and is there an Irish culture worth mentioning, or just a lot of hairy strands of Irish cultures, and are we Europeans at all at all or part of the American main, and does it matter and so on to the end of boredom. I heard someone quip that our summer schools really only amount to one theme: 'The English were here and now they are gone.'

There is still, of course, that great fund of goodwill out there to be tapped. Most people still have a loyalty to the language, even if it is purely sentimental, merely 'a low intensity aspiration' to coin Conor Cruise O'Brien's pithy phrase. Very few are actively hostile, although many are positively indifferent. Others profess real love for the language, but as soon as any measure is proposed that may enhance it, they will beg to oppose. People like the fact that it is out there, but feel uncomfortable when it is spoken in their presence. We are a truly mixed-up people. The language is taught throughout the republican state to nearly all pupils from infants up to Leaving Certificate. This is often done with brilliance and enthusiasm, and often with a watery dribble, and often with everything in between. We spend a great deal of energy trying to get people to learn it, but make it next to impossible for them to use it outside the classroom. The state funded Bord na Gaeilge for years, but its recommendations vanished into a paper hole somewhere in the middle of the civil service; language policy now receives direction from a cross-border body, Foras na Gaeilge, so that we at present reside in a stranger limbo still where the British government have a large say in what we can do!

I remain one of 'the band of hope and glory' that Máirtín Ó Cadhain used to excoriate. This is not because I expect any miracles like the one that already brought the language back from the brink of the grave. It is because I believe that there isn't much else of substance left in the identity kitty, and for all our much-vaunted bits and bobs and blotches and blobs of a varied and macular and spotted and patchy inclusive 'culture', if 'Irish' identity is to mean anything at all, it must mean something in the first place. Most of the other props have melted away. Synge's strange suggestion that we should be transbegorrifying

Hiberno-English into a national tongue does be after going down with the sun that bees kissing the puckered hem of the sea over Galway bay. Catholicism, or nay also Christianity, even in its post-Vatican II easy-peasy lite version no longer calls the faithful to prayer and allegiance. Literature and music and the arts stay in the margins for Saturday night at the movies or the concert hall and for a book at bedtime or the summer beach. Only sport shakes its locks as something that brings people together in some kind of national communion.

Right now, at this moment in time, as the cliché has it, it would be difficult to recover that first carefree rapture of discovery that marked the Irish revival and largely defined the Irish Free State. Right now, at this moment in time, it would be difficult for any state with liberal and plural pretensions in an open society to undertake a big social project with vigour: there isn't much enthusiasm to solve the very solvable social problems of a small tiny black unvelveted band of itinerants, to pluck one random example from the caravanserai of life, not to mention a language question that involves the whole community. Right now, at this moment in time, to joyfully misquote Kavanagh's awful poem, 'culture is always something that was/ something that economists measure.'

But what is absolutely certain, is that where we are now, is not where we are going to be in the next generation. Mící Mac Gabhann wrote of '*rotha mór an tsaoil*'; Johnny Cash sang that the man comes round. There is always a future. The point is to do something about it.

The Sound Within

Kate Fennell

I don't know how old I was when I realised that it wasn't only people with brown eyes that spoke that other strange language which I didn't understand. I must have been around seven, because it was at that point that we left Maoinis Island, Conamara, and moved to the metropolis of Galway. There I noticed that even the people with grey, blue and green eyes, the same as my friends' and family's, spoke this language. The two brown-eyed brothers in Maoinis school, known as the 'come-day-go-days' because of their frequent excursions to a faraway country called Thurles, had been the only children I had known until then who spoke and understood fluent English. I was soon to be immersed in this language and my family home was to become an island of Irish. Well, not entirely because my new city school had a rule which meant that we were not allowed to speak English. Yet they had difficulty understanding my Irish.

The language police would circulate in the *clós* during break-times noting down the names of people who were singing the skipping rhyme 'Vote, vote, vote for de Valera' in English. I couldn't win. I was proud now to be beginning to converse in this new language but already it was a crime. While, at the same time, my Irish was the cause of much mirth since I pronounced guttural 'ch' with much more of an 'ach' sound than they. While their 'chs' were rendered as 'ks', mine were softer and more like the 'ch' in the Scottish 'Loch Ness'. Teachers would not hesitate to make me stand up in class and speak to my new classmates in my native tongue so that they could hear this beautiful Irish. I didn't know what they found beautiful about my rough accent, as I saw it. The language I was learning was a lot cleaner and less wild. All I knew was that I never had any difficulty with those *'agam, agat, aiges'* and spelling tests were easy. What did cause me confusion though was *madra, tonnta, ag dul, páistí, ag cur fearthainne, tar anseo!* and other phrases and verbs. My equivalents were *gadhar, maidhmeanna, ag gabháil, gasúir, ag scréachadh (báistí)* and *gabh i leith!* respectively. I started to get the feeling that my Irish was wrong. I should be saying these words that were in the book. Their pronunciation of my language was totally different too. A slight feeling of shame and embarassment began to creep into my psyche. Why do I speak this language so differently from them? No child wants to be different, but as soon as I would open my mouth in class the difference would be as plain as day.

Language is sound. It is the first sound that reverberates in the human body. The mouth and the vocal chords shape these words that we utter. It is not grammar, syntax, or old, middle or modern. It doesn't know borders or religions and it has no sense of time. It is the coming together of the mind, heart, and physical body to communicate with the world around us, which since time immemorial has been inhabited by humans. Therefore it is the most common tool that humans use to communicate with one another. Apparently language was not always there. As cavepeople we grunted and made noises to suit our intentions. Our way of communication now is the same but more sophisticated. It is still a basic expression of the human being.

Songs seem to carry these expressions most effectively over generations and geographical distances. Each tribe has dirges, each tribe has songs of victory, of pure joy, of love, of longing and so on. Song is a translation of feeling and thought into sound so as to communicate more directly with the heart and soul of others. When this is successful we often get the meaning without understanding the words. The sound suffices to close the gap between language and understanding.

When I was uprooted from Conamara, the world of sounds that I knew vanished almost completely. I started to make new sounds. They were crisper, sharper, harder and varied less in tone than my native tongue. There was a handful of people that I knew who spoke native Irish like me. Each time we would converse I felt that we were excluding others because very often they would be left with blank faces. With English it was the contrary. Everybody understood me when I spoke. It was inclusive. It could be a beautiful language in poetry and prose. But the sound of it never became my sound, I felt. It felt alien to me.

In my life today these are the sounds I have to make to be understood in the main. But they don't make me feel whole. I feel I am speaking from my head. When I speak Irish I feel I am speaking from my heart. It is not surprising, therefore, that I was drawn to the Slavic languages to find the sounds that I missed. Russian has those 'shhs' and 'chs' and 'nyas' and thick consonants that I was used to mouthing from a young age. It is an old, rich and very poetic language. I fell in love with this language, learnt it, lived in Russia and felt that a hole had been considerably filled. After all, you can live there and everyone speaks it, not just in a pocket somewhere where there is little employment and a dependence on grants, but everywhere and, importantly, they are proud of it. Yet the gnawing feeling of lacking something was to return later and twenty years after leaving Conamara I returned for my fix. I wanted to live in a world where my original sounds were understood not by a select few but by everyone from the postman to the county councillor. I didn't want to be seen as a freak for speaking this 'dead language' as I had often felt while studying and living in Dublin. I wanted to hear the same sounds returned. Now my heart was singing in earnest. I had needed to be reconnected. The fact that it was an emotional experience as much as a linguistic one was not lost on me.

In Ireland, Irish is more of an emotional question than a linguistic one. The sound of Irish seems to be lodged in the subconscious mind of our people. That might explain why discussions about Irish are more of an emotional nature than about the intricacies of the language itself. If I had a service which gave a listening ear to those who wanted to vent their frustration, disappointment and anger at the way Irish was taught to them in school I would be able to retire now on the profits. If, on the other hand, each payment was withdrawn when someone told me how they loved Irish and how they wished they could speak it or were attending nightclasses or were foreign but had learnt it like a native, well I'm afraid I would then be back where I started. It is such an emotionally-charged subject in Ireland it nearly ceases to be seen as a European language with a culture and a history as unique as Spanish or Portuguese. The fact that Irish is the third oldest written European language after Greek and Latin seldom arises as part of a discussion about Irish. It's the longing to know it or the very hatred of it. Rarely is there apathy towards it. Never is there as much emotion expressed in relation to the other languages they failed to learn at school or didn't enjoy – and even less knowledge about them. The sounds that I made as a child are still ringing in our ears and pounding in our hearts waiting to be released.

This was highlighted for me recently when I was asked to say a Prayer of the Faithful in Irish at a friend's wedding. The congregation was reading from their pamphlets in English and when I uttered the short prayer in Irish there was some surprise. Nothing could have prepared me for what happened afterwards. If I ever felt what it was like to be a popstar, well I had my moment then. The amount of congratulations and gushing praise that I received could have been equal to that of an MTV award-winner. There were outbursts such as, 'Oh it's so beautiful to hear the Irish spoken; such a beautiful sound!' 'Oh your Irish is beautiful!' 'Oh I wish I could speak it! I've forgotten it all. I used to love it at school!' or 'My teacher was terrible at school' and so on. Barely thirty seconds of Irish had eclipsed two hours of English. I wished I could have given them more or waved a wand so that their Irish would come flooding effortlessly back and this barrier from ourselves would be lifted. These are the moments when being an Irish-speaker is a warm feeling. Yet it is not always so.

I fear there are many misperceptions about native Irish-speakers in Ireland today. Broadly speaking, this situation seems to arise out of a misunderstanding between those who live in the Gaeltacht and those, to use an Irish-language term, who live in the *Galltacht*, i.e. those who have been brought up in an English-speaking area and speak English in the home. This gap is rapidly being reduced because of the proliferation of *gaelscoileanna*, the popularity of TG4, our growing confidence and improved economic climate. The end result of this is that the stigma of speaking Irish has lessened, but confusion between the camps still remains.

I've witnessed many people in the *Galltacht* expressing the belief that Gaeltacht people have a real sense of pride about their language and would prefer to keep the 'blow-ins' out. This may be true of some, but the truth is that a feeling of inferiority is rampant among native Irish-speakers and has been for centuries. If, as I have previously alluded, hundreds of years of its existence has penetrated our psyche and and continues to draw us towards it, equally the hundreds of years of persecution and suffering linked with it have left their indelible mark on Irish-speakers in the Gaeltacht today. Many instances have made this plain to me.

For example, several years ago, I was a wandering spectator at an outdoor event during an Irish language festival, Pléaráca Chonamara, in the heart of Conamara. A local woman, within earshot of me, was reprimanding her young child. It may be surprising to know that the language she used with her child was English even though she normally spoke Irish. You could tell by her quite broken English that she rarely had reason to speak it. I got the impression that she used English because I, a stranger whom she mistook for an English-speaking 'blow-in', was standing nearby. Instead of feeling proud that her mother tongue and everyday language was Irish she appeared to feel ashamed of it. I approached her and made chit-chat about the weather in Irish. She was taken aback but smiled and answered me in Irish.

English is felt to be the 'better' language by many in the Gaeltacht. The teenagers speak English while they are eating their sandwiches outside the local shop at lunchtime in Carraroe. They speak English when they are playing in the yard. On saluting a stranger in Conamara, English is more often than not the language used. There is a shyness about using the language unless we are sure the other person converses in it comfortably. Amongst the younger generation English is considered cool, Irish not. In the past English meant being educated and getting on in life. Understandably, it is hard to shake off those shackles.

Usually, in a circle of Irish speakers, if one person who doesn't speak the language joins the group, the conversation will turn to English. This, of course, changes the dynamic. It feels strange for me to speak English to my siblings or to close friends whose native language is Irish. But because we are bilingual and communication is the key, the minority language gets dropped sooner. It is the lesser of the two in practical life and so has a very fragile existence even on a daily basis. For a language to thrive there has to be a feeling of it being equal to any other language around it.

The bridge between the Gaeltacht and the *Galltacht* is a wide one and Irish has often been looked upon as the poor cousin. Certainly when I was on the receiving end of the comment recently at a party 'You speak Irish and you're not a geek?!', I realised the gulf between the two worlds was far too wide for any *Bille Teanga* or well-meaning Minister for the Gaeltacht to narrow. In brief, Irish comes with baggage. And so there was only one thing for the ugly duckling to do.

I still had my *blas* when I returned to live in Conamara for a few years, which meant that after the preliminary round of questioning to ascertain my stock, I was treated like one of their own. I don't think I would have had the same experience if I had been a non-native speaker from, let's say, Tipperary. That is natural. A language is not simply the words you say to someone else to convey a message. There is a whole attitude and way of expressing yourself that is unique to that language. Each language has its own nuances, from particular words to body language to the type of humour that belongs to that language. Similarly with Irish, our points of reference are different to that in the English-speaking world. We have different heroes, different connections and a different vocabulary. Words themselves and how they are used is something that the ordinary person pays attention to everyday when speaking. They are the tools we use to construct the image of ourselves that we would like reflected for others. As a result, I think it's true to say that we feel and express ourselves differently when speaking different languages.

Interestingly, when I am in England or in central Europe, even though I speak and understand their languages I don't feel that connection with them that I feel when I travel to countries further east. The Eastern outlook on life sits more comfortably with me than that of the continent or Northern Europe. I always feel that the people further east are more like people from Irish-speaking Conamara. Equally, I feel more at home in Mediterranean countries than in English-speaking ones. I have pondered this and tried to work out why this is so. As we know, the roots of our language are not Germanic or Nordic nor even descended from Latin. If it is true that Irish is a Celtic language, a tribe that is believed to have had origins near Czech and up as far as the Black Sea, then it seems that a language carries with it more than sounds. The language reflects the way the people think, feel and see their place in the world. Generations of shaping the language means generations of people sharing a simliar world-view which their language serves to put across. English cannot express us in the same way because it has been shaped by different peoples who adored different gods. We have undoubtedly shaped the English that was brought here and everyday I hear expressions which are direct translations from the Irish.

Yet, on more than one occasion, I have met people who feel cheated because their native language is English and not Irish. Deep down they feel Irish is their language but they do not speak it. English doesn't seem to serve its purpose for them when they try to express who they are. It seems our native tongue has a grasp on us that even we cannot comprehend.

Personally, I often wish I only had one native language. It would simplify my internal and external worlds. As it is, I feel I am living in two cultures. If I would like to participate in the world that understands *sean-nós*, tradition, turns-of-phrase in Irish, lyrical descriptions of the landscape I grew up in, well then I would be living in the Irish-speaking world, which means the Gaeltacht. If on the other hand I would like to be a part of a lively, young, modern, fast-changing city-life then I would be living in an English-speaking world or abroad where Irish is not the everyday sound. To live in either culture involves a decisive geographical choice which leaves me feeling split in two.

I sometimes try to join the two by attending Irish-language events in the city or going to places where the music and traditions are alive, but I'm afraid it doesn't fulfil me. It exaggerates that feeling of being a dinosaur in an oasis. Along with that the Irish that is learnt in the *Galltacht, an caighdeán oifigiúil*, differs considerably from my native tongue. It differs in terms of sound and vocabulary. It's rare that someone has the same richness and fluency if they haven't had the opportunity to spend time in a Gaeltacht. Sometimes I feel that it impedes real deep communication in Irish because I am aware that our sounds are different and there are grammar mistakes to overlook and so on. I cannot fully relax in the conversation because I am aware I could use an expression that they may not know and then it turns into a language class when all I want to do is converse with my fellow countrymen and women!

Native Irish also has its own inherent music which is mostly missing from the *caighdeán oifigiúil*. English sounds are much thinner than the Irish so it is often difficult for an English-speaker to make them. My great sadness is that the music and the richness of the language is dying with the native speakers and the new language pronounces its 'chs' as 'ks'. No-one is to blame, it is simply the way things are.

I am aware that as I write the above, Irish could be substituted with Konkani or Ruthenian or any of the minority languages in the world which are dying off faster than species of insects if you believe the newspapers and the linguists. It is not unique to Ireland. In fact what is unique these days compared to the ancient past is that most of us are monolingual. The rich tapestry of accents and dialects in Ireland tells of a much more varied linguistic plateau in times gone by. In many countries this is true today. Although we now only have two, the language question in Ireland is still a complex one. I watch the *Nuacht* sometimes and wonder how it must feel not to be able to understand the reader who is speaking what is purportedly the first official language of the country. I am sure many English-speakers feel let down by the way Irish was taught to them in school. Personally, I feel privileged to know Irish from my birth and for it to have been shaped by the rocks and rough seas of Conamara. It has certainly made my world richer.

It is also strange to be living in a time when the language of my birth is by all appearances dying, a culture dying with it. One may ask, why bother to save this language which is perhaps for many nothing more than a nostalgic vestige of the past? Maybe because Irish is our sound. Passed on from our ancestors, it is ingrained in the crevices of the monastery walls, Viking ports, Norman castles, thatched cottages and even the luxury duplexes. All we have to do is look at our placenames and know that every hillock was baptised by the people who lived and worked the land for hundreds of years. They had an intimate knowledge of and a communion with their surroundings. Just as our ecosystem changes when another species dies so too does our conscious world when a language, which is the key to an entire culture, dies. The effect of losing our language is a subtle shift in our harmony with ourselves. It will not make headlines, but its survival is necessary for our fundamental feeling of belonging and our understanding of who we really are.

A Dangerous Silence

Neasa Ní Chinnéide

It was the year I had made my First Communion, and I was allowed one of the major treats in our lives at the time – a holiday in Dublin. It was a magic place to me, full of aunts and cousins, Nelson's Pillar and the Number 7 bus where I could get an eyeful of the sights of O'Connell Street from the front seats at the top. It would be hard to describe the excitement of the trip from Kerry on the train. For a start, I could actually taste the city some miles before we got into Heuston Station because of the smoky air. It seemed to me to be a romantic sort of tang, promising footpaths to roller-skate on, Kylemore cakes and the pictures. Once when I was really lucky there was a bus strike and there were soldiers to swing you in and out of trucks instead of buses.

On the Friday after my arrival my aunt dispatched my cousins and myself to the church nearby for Confessions. The major difficulty at the time was figuring out some nice interesting sin to tell. Our parish priest at home at the time was very elderly and quite deaf, and if you went to him at the top of the church (he sitting on a chair in the sacristy, head turned away so he was not looking directly at the sinner) you could hear a very interesting variety of possibilities to inspire you as you waited your turn. This was a good option if you did not feel you had anything grievous enough to tell the curate in the 'real' confessional, but I had been in that kind of confessional before and felt reasonably confident of this one. So, in I went. I felt a certain amount of anxiety as the wooden sliding door above me moved across with a gentle thud to reveal the priest. 'Now my child.' I froze. The awful truth dawned on me. *He was speaking in English.*

I was seized by a great desire just to make a run for it. But then a flash of inspiration hit me and I remembered the sermon our curate had preached at Christmastime when all the emigrants were home. *'Is cuma le Dia cén teanga a labhrann tú.'* Mustering up such courage as I could, I launched forth into my confession in the only language I had for the job: *'Beannaigh mé, a Athair, de bhrí gur pheacaíos.'* 'Get out!' thundered the voice. 'Get out and stop mocking me!'

I said nothing to my aunt after this event, and went on, in the merry way of children, to forget all about it (almost). Later, I would think about it as I lay considering things before I fell asleep. Most people I knew spoke two languages without giving it much thought. Some people only spoke one, but that one generally was not English. Some people spoke *Gaeilge agus Béarla.* Even in the nearby town where I knew there were houses we could speak *Gaeilge* in (and many more houses where we might not) I never had the thought that people could not *understand.* But I kept these thoughts to myself and never told anybody about what had happened in Dublin.

Later on, I wondered why my name was in English on my birth certificate. It was explained to me that the nurse who wrote it down in the nursing home where I was born simply refused to write my name in Irish. This type of daily response on a habitual basis contributed to a situation where people no longer felt empowered to assert their basic instincts in respect of identity. Outside certain circles, the real truth was that Irish was not considered quite respectable. To this day, those of us who have Irish names will frequently get asked 'What's that in English?' This never happens when you are visiting another country. Your name is just a name, and rarely causes a fuss apart from people wondering how it might be pronounced. Where did we get the *mentalité* that produces such a result? And what are the personal consequences which, multiplied by a lifetime's experiences, become social and political consequences to a people for whom this has been a common experience? This short essay looks at aspects of these issues based to some extent – as such things must necessarily be – on my own life and my understanding of the lives of people of my acquaintance in an Irish-speaking community. I am particularly interested in these choices in the context of what linguists are saying about language today. What value does language have in itself? At the wider end of the lens, what is the likely outcome of the European Union experiment in respect of our individual cultures as expressed through language? The latter is a big question and we will only be able to give it the briefest of consideration, but the fact is that Ireland is a country which punches above its weight in many respects, and our recent economic success has made us an inspiration and a subject of much debate and scrutiny among that group of nations who are, as I write, about to join the EU in the near and mid-term future. What we do in respect of our own language is a matter of some consequence.

The world I grew up in was of course a bilingual world, as the Gaeltacht has been for a very long time. Some people only spoke English, particularly some mothers or fathers from elsewhere who had married a Gaeltacht person. Many in my village had lived for a period in another country before returning to live at home. Most people could speak English well, as they would have needed to in order to gain employment, or could at least express themselves reasonably well. But all the children could speak Irish, and the daily language of my parish was – and remains for the most part – Irish. It is the magic of the place for me; the pleasure of it is sensual. The strange thing is that you might visit this place and not realise it was so. This is because as soon as a stranger comes amongst us, people will speak English. Visitors who actually speak Irish find this intensely irritating, and those who come in the expectation of hearing what Irish sounds like find it disappointing. It has led some observers to conclude that Irish is in danger of becoming a 'private' language.[1]

The situation I have described has also led to a seriously damaging discourse in the public press. People in letters columns and some opinion columns regularly declare the language to be a thing of no importance, or defunct, or some combination of both. There are occasionally some ripostes, usually of a defensive kind. The vast body of the people are silent. I have begun to understand that this is a dangerous silence, because into such a silence creeps all kinds of opportunities for ignorance and bad policy to flourish.

There are wider implications involved in this debate. If we cannot understand the dynamic involved in language courtesy and respect, we stand in danger of showing an equal lack of understanding of the by now reasonably large segment of our population that is from other lands. There are important common components at the heart of both. Permission to be different is at the heart of the decision of parents with Irish-speaking children to raise them truly bilingually, for no parent will willingly expose a child to opprobrium. A confident parent may be willing to battle the odds, but for anybody even slightly at a disadvantage, the choice becomes one that is very difficult. Many parents in the Gaeltacht have found themselves in a dilemma in this respect, as it has not been made clear to people that the important thing is to learn well in one language, and that the additional language skills will follow. It has been up to individual teachers to reassure parents on this score, but there has not been a general reassurance about the attainability of full bilingualism.

It is important to recognise that the context in a Gaeltacht is materially different than that, for example, in a *gaelscoil* environment in an English-speaking area. Many schools in the Gaeltacht today feel torn between the demands of parents who are monolingual in English and the linguistic needs of the others in the community. The absence of a clear state policy on the language in recent decades, decades which have seen in-migration into Gaeltacht areas for economic reasons, have led to a lack of empowerment or social consensus in favour of education in the communal language. There are parents who come into Gaeltacht areas armed with the view that the language of the community is not important to them, and that their rights are not being vindicated if they cannot have their children educated locally in English. This is a powerful dagger in the heart of a community where the language choice is coming under other pressures. Conversely, there are people moving into Gaeltacht areas who value the language; such people work creatively within the community bringing in new skills and ideas and actually strengthen the community's commitment and self-esteem. Among them are people whose own mother tongue is not English; unburdened by traditional attitudes, they rarely evince a difficulty with the acquisition of Irish – it is just another language.

It seems to me that a rebuilding of a societal consensus about bilinguality and its merits is the most important 'front-end' aspect of any debate and policy about Irish-English bilingualism in Ireland. Healthy bilingualism is a state in which two languages are seen as complementary, not in competition-fulfilling different roles, with each language being seen in a rewarding light.[2] Without this consensus and the 'permission' it brings, very little may come of recent initiatives at state level such as the Official Languages Act 2003 other than moans of complaint about more tokenism. The rebuilding of a social consensus means moving away from a debate between those who are in entrenched positions on both side of a divide, and from a view of Irish as a language whose value is judged within a framework which views its revival as merely a nationalist project of the last century.[3] It is equally important not to delude ourselves with the notion that the preservation of certain aspects of culture such as crafts or music are sufficient in themselves.

Music, painting, crafts, and other forms of cultural expression all play their part: but language plays the largest part of all.[4] It is worth reminding ourselves that in the history of the world, monolingualism has generally been the exception:

> ... the world is a mosaic of visions. With each language that disappears, a piece of that mosaic is lost.[5]

We have been behaving as if our Hiberno-English is a robust enough vessel to contain our experience as a people. Its hitherto enduring power and beauty as witnessed in recent works such as John McGahern's *That They May Face the Rising Sun* is extraordinary. The book is redolent of the Irish language among other major influences evident in the speech of its protagonists. But will this richness continue to endure? As we listen to the speech of our children, what we hear is increasingly Anglo-American. The phrases and words hitherto common in our English are being transformed, in the normal way of language, through time. If we want to hear our own voices from the past informing our increasingly confident future, can we really presume that we will retain a full vision of who we were and may be without recourse to the well-spring from which we came?

It is interesting that at the academic level the most recent debate has surrounded the issue of filling university chairs in mediaeval Irish departments. While this is an area of enormous importance, representing the means of deepening our knowledge and making a true cultural understanding of the past possible, the necessity as a proximate project to recognise the need for 'joined-up thinking' on the issue of the survival of Irish as a vernacular must take precedence at the leading edge of the debate. There is current evidence of a deep-seated wish on the part of many people in this society to repossess the patrimony of Irish, as evidenced in the support for the *gaelscoileanna* movement, now celebrating a quarter-century of growth, the proliferation of local language-learning groups, the emergence of initiatives to socialise on a bilingual basis in the cities – the list goes on. Research indicates that one of the motives among English-speaking parents of children who have sought to have Irish-medium education in the Republic of Ireland is that the greatest advantage resulting from the decision to make Irish the language of the home is seen as enhanced linguistic competence.[6] This choice is a highway, not a cul-de-sac.

Underpinning it is a basic structural fact; not since the Middle Ages has the spread of social classes with an ability to speak the language to one degree or another been as wide, given the upward mobility of people in a rapidly developing economy. It is a shallower hold of course, but it is significant that it coincides with a palpable feeling of cultural confidence. Confidence and will have frequently been factors in the trajectory of languages.[7] It coincides with a wider public space in which the language is visible, provided in the most recent decades by the growth of the Irish-language media. It also coincides with a remarkable new era in which the power of the individual is in some senses at an all-time high, a theme explored at some length in the discussion of the globalisation issue by Thomas Friedman.[8] This is particularly true in the access to distance learning over the internet, and to the sound of our languages as our radio stations can broadcast by satellite all over the globe. People in South America listen to Catalan radio on the computer; people all over the world can hear Raidió na Gaeltachta. As I write, a truly remarkable language-learning tool for Irish is about to be launched on the market, pioneered by an ex-employee of IBM who, frustrated at the difficulty of sourcing such material to revisit and improve the Irish-language skills he acquired in childhood, decided to devise one himself.

Many of these initiatives – including the one I have just instanced, have received some state money via the channels that exist. But it is significant that the front-end of the impetus in the last quarter-century has been from individuals driven to find solutions for themselves. Whatever the general public perception may be, the fight for our language is coming from deep within the hearts of many people. These trends have been noted as a remarkable sign of hope and vitality and they are; the challenge for today is to create an overarching paradigm for what the state, on the one hand, is trying to achieve and the individual efforts of persons and organisations on the other.

One of the first things we have to concentrate on is the statement of a goal that is realistic, attainable and attuned to the way we live now. For people like me, returning to the *status quo* of my childhood world is no longer possible. Like many other Gaeltacht people, I live somewhere else. But far more opportunities now exist to live in our own country, whether that means never having to leave it, or leaving it and returning. We have seen how other countries handle language, as we know that bilingualism and multilingualism are normal and acceptable in societies across the globe.[9] Speaking *Gaeilge agus Béarla* is not the seventh wonder of the world, nor is it necessary to choose between them. We can speak both, and more. We can and increasingly do raise our children to be bilingual and encourage them to learn other languages as well. We do have a dilemma in that it is clear that a language that does not have some defined geographical base is at a great disadvantage. The people of the Gaeltacht areas themselves put forward a great number of eminently practical solutions to help resolve these problems.[10] For all of the speakers of Irish, there has to be a general approach that the wider society will understand. From those who do not speak a word to those with the *cúpla focal* to the fluent, we need a plan that allows them to feel that they have a right to be part of such a linguistically-flexible society, whether actively as speakers or only as listeners who wish to eavesdrop and enjoy.

One issue to be dealt with is the general area of language courtesy. We have been caught in a self-defeating cycle of making our language 'disappear', as I discussed earlier. We have generally only spoken it when we know in advance that the person we are conversing with speaks Irish. In the most extreme cases, people have developed the habit of only conversing with people who speak their particular dialect; hence I have gone into a shop in Conamara and asked for a selection of goods in fluent Kerry Irish, only to have the person at the cash register (whom I have just heard conversing in fluent Irish) answer me in English. We are becoming conscious that this is a discourtesy, considerably assisted by the mutual intelligibility of our dialects which has been fostered by Raidió na Gaeltachta in particular over the last quarter-century.

The trends toward repossessing Irish through the internet, in our communities, in the *gaelscoil* system and in the media are a remarkable sign of hope and vitality, but the challenge is to make systematic steps toward encouraging people to use the language skills they have in their everyday lives and in public as well as in private. The Official Languages Act 2003, which is in the process of being implemented, has addressed some important aspects of a response from the state in the area of re-conferring on the language the status it has enshrined in our constitution. Its focus is primarily on the provision of state services through Irish. It is also necessary now to undo the badly thought-out decision not to look for official status for the language at the level of the European Union. State policy needs to be consistent on language rights, and this made even more important by the undoubted status Ireland has earned among those states which are about to accede to a new status as full members of the European Union.

While the status the Official Languages Act confers on Irish in public life is a step in the right direction, it will be difficult to persuade the state employees in the wide-ranging panoply of organisations charged with its delivery to be truly motivated if there is not a public willing to engage with them. The public interested in Irish needs the clear restatement in a new millennium as to why the constitutional position of Irish is worth defending, preferably in the context of the stated European respect for cultural diversity. We also need a tolerance of the processes of linguistic change that have occurred in Irish as a language in the last century. Linguist James McCloskey has pointed out that while the form of *Gaeilge* which is emerging may fall well short of the ideals of Conradh na Gaeilge at its foundation in the nineteenth century, it has been a very substantial and remarkable achievement nonetheless.

It follows also, if we view the situation of Irish in the perspective of global language endangerment, that we cannot be too fussy at the kind of language that emerges at the end of this strange experiment.[11]

There was a time in my life when I might have scorned such a conclusion. But what am I to say to the small children whose voices I hear in the urban *gaelscoil* yard? Or those who have never had my chance to be totally immersed in a linguistic culture steeped in the songs and lore of centuries?

We should be encouraged by the practice of other societies to understand that people use languages for many purposes, and we do not have to use each all the time. As the poet Michael Hartnett pointed out rather sagely, English is a good language to sell pigs in. It may indeed be a good language for the market, or as a *lingua franca* – and in our hands it has been more. It has been the language of Dublin for as long as it has been the language of London. It has been a key element of our economic growth. But we can use Irish for a different set of purposes, to affirm important parts of who we are and discover again the shores of who we were and might be. A living language repossessed has all these possibilities; it can hearken back as well as forward, enriching itself as it goes. Once gone, these doors shut firmly behind us.

Why is this so important? It is important in the first instance because of what was aptly observed by the historian Louis Cullen many years ago; in Ireland, *real* tradition is rather thinner on the ground than we might wish to believe.[12] We have many truncated traditions owing to the trajectory of our history. Traditional music has lead to new flowerings, and we are enthusiastically partaking in popular culture. But as to the unbroken threads that characterise many other countries in art, music, dance, cuisine, architecture, we are in our infancy. We have almost eradicated vernacular architecture. Visual art is only beginning to reassert itself at the broad popular level. There are huge gaps between the past of archaeology and the living heritage of contemporary culture.

One of the very few continuous and unique threads that bind us to who we were and are today is the Irish language. Who will we be? What voice will we have? What will stand out about us as a unique culture with its own special inspiration and characteristics? I am reminded of a conversation that I had a number of years ago in Tokyo. I was speaking about Ireland to a Japanese neighbour. 'But you hardly have a distinctive culture,' she observed. I spoke of our literature – Yeats, Joyce, music and so on. She listened for a while. Then she said, 'Yes. But do you have a *language?*'

We do. We have something real and unique. As historians and poets and linguists do not tire of telling us, the language we use tells a tale of what the life journeys of all our ancestors have been, a treasure-trove, a key to pasts and futures. The researches of linguists in the last two decades underscore the importance of language diversity in keeping alive the widest understanding of what human experience encompasses in an increasingly globalised world. Now, as we sit on the threshold of a brighter future than those who first considered the idea of language revival ever thought possible, let us not let the moment pass. Let us avoid the dangerous silence.

Notes

1 Glyn Williams, 'From Diagnosis to Cure: Euromosaic, Language and Economic Development' in Pádraig Ó Riagáin and Síle Harrington (eds), *A Language Strategy for Europe – Retrospect and Prospect*, Bord na Gaeilge, 1999.
2 David Crystal, *Language Death*, Cambridge University Press, 2000, p. 81.
3 On this, one of the recent more thoughtful voices has been James McCloskey, *Voices Silenced: Has Irish a Future?*, Cois Life, Dublin, 2001.
4 Crystal, *ibid.*, p. 39.
5 François Grosjean, *Life with Two Languages*, Harvard University Press, 1982, (quoted in Crystal, *ibid.*, p. 45.)
6 David Singleton, Síle Harrington and Alison Henry, *At the sharp end of language revival: English-speaking parents raising Irish-speaking children*, CLCS Occasional Paper No. 57, Trinity College Dublin, 2000.
7 For a general discussion, see for example, Tore Janson, *Speak – a Short History of Languages*, Oxford University Press, 2002.
8 See the introduction in Thomas L. Friedman, *Longitudes and Attitudes*, Farrar, Straus and Giroux, New York, 2002.
9 Crystal, *ibid.*, p. 134.
10 *Tuairisc Choimisiún na Gaeltachta*, commissioned under the aegis of the Department of Community, Rural and Gaeltacht Affairs, 2002.
11 McCloskey, *ibid.*, p. 47.
12 L.M. Cullen, *The Emergence of Modern Ireland, 1600-1900*, Batsford Academic Press, 1981. Cf. chapter 6, particularly pp. 136-9.

Níl Sí Doiligh a Iompar!
No Load to Carry

A personal response to the current situation of Irish

Lillis Ó Laoire

'Irish is in danger.' 'Irish is more alive than ever.' 'The future of Irish needs to be carefully planned.' 'Irish is a waste of time, money and effort.' These are some statements that can be heard about Irish in Ireland. I agree strongly with the first two and acknowledge that a significant number of people identify with the last two of these statements, although not all are willing to do so publicly. I grew up speaking Irish and English in an Irish-speaking part of Donegal, a Gaeltacht, indeed a *fíor-Ghaeltacht* in the terminology of the 1926 Commission at whose hearings both my great-grandfather, and his son-in-law, my grandfather, gave oral testimony.

'Language planning' is a phrase often heard nowadays, since Minister Éamon Ó Cuív's initiative which introduced the first Official Languages Act into law in July 2003. This measure is crucial in order to protect areas where Irish still has any currency as a vernacular, and also to lend support in places where people are trying to establish new bilingual communities, where a more than token use of Irish forms part of a language choice which is consciously and deliberately embraced. Many of these are springing up around newly established *gaelscoileanna*. The prototype for them is probably the Shaw's Road community established in Belfast in the 1960s.

As a measure of inclusion, we need to remember and revitalise the older meaning of the word Gaeltacht. Originally, this meant Irish- or Gaelic-speaking people wherever they might be found. It applied to people and to networks of communication. It gradually became identified with parts of the country, a process cemented by the Gaeltacht Commission in 1926.

Language planning has a longer history on this island than most people realise. The deliberate policy of using English only in all official business was fostered by the colonial state from the seventeenth century onwards. The great sixteenth-century English poet and colonist, Edmund Spenser, recognised that 'the speech being Irish, the heart must needs be Irish'. In his view, a change of language was seen as a necessary element in the campaign to subdue and pacify Ireland and its people, and this aim was deliberately and single-mindedly pursued. Later, in the 1830s, in a continuation of this official policy, Irish was excluded from the curriculum of the new national schools, and was even forbidden as a means of instruction for children who were coming to school with no knowledge of English, although bilingual teachers must have often ignored this rule in practice. It should be remembered that Ireland at this time had, at a very conservative estimate, up to two million speakers of the language, so that the exclusion was a planned action. It may have been carried out with the best of intentions, to provide a 'good' basic education for some of the poorest sections of the Irish population, giving them a knowledge of English and bringing them out of their backwardness into the so-called modern world. It was also, however, a denial of a fundamental human right. The catastrophe of the Great Famine struck a devastating blow to Irish-speakers, many of whom were, after all, among the most disadvantaged sections of society. Although the decline of the language had begun perhaps as early as the sixteenth century, as a consequence of inimical state policies, it was the Great Famine of the 1840s that dramatically accelerated the abandonment of Irish. Most people correctly saw the language as an obstacle to material advancement in a world increasingly dominated by emigration to England, its colonies and the United States.

Partly due to the galloping language shift starkly evident in post-Famine Ireland, the revival of interest in Ireland's indigenous culture became increasingly concerned with linguistic matters as the nineteenth century wore on. The Society for the Preservation of the Irish Language first, and later the Gaelic League, sought to arrest this dramatic decline and to revitalise Irish in areas where it was still the dominant vernacular. Although often viewed negatively only in terms of (backward-looking) romantic nationalism, these movements were much more than that. The activists of the Gaelic League, in particular, had a poetic vision rather than a rationally-based, empirically-researched and scientifically-validated 'plan' that might be used today, but nevertheless it had powerful effects. Indeed, I am convinced that this vision impinged directly upon my own life and history and I remain grateful for its influence.

The national reawakening, spearheaded by the Gaelic League and its outgrowth, Coláiste Uladh, the Irish-language college founded in Gortahork in Donegal in 1906, and the later establishment of the state in 1921, succeeded in significantly retarding the decline of Irish in my area. A pattern of language shift over three generations was the norm in Ireland in the nineteenth and indeed into the twentieth century. Although numerous exceptions existed, typically, two monoglot Irish-speaking parents would see to it that their children could speak English. The second bilingual generation would then, in turn, transmit only English to its own children. Often the second generation understood Irish, but could not or was unwilling to speak it. Regarded within this pattern, my mother's generation should have been the one to have become English-speaking only. After all, her own mother, my grandmother, Mary McFadden (1899-1968), spoke English by preference. Although I cannot really remember what language I used with my grandmother, since she died when I was very young, I remember her sister, my great-aunt Sally (1901-1981), who also lived in Gortahork, very clearly. Although she spoke Irish well, she preferred to speak English, and we normally used English when speaking to her. She used Irish mostly with casual acquaintances from the locality who sometimes called in to visit, and who preferred mostly to speak Irish. Born at the turn of the twentieth century into a middle-class business family, her language choice was not unusual, as English was then not merely an instrument of communication, but a symbol of social prestige. There were other reasons why English was preferred in the McFadden household. Their own grandmother, Mary Robinson, had been an English-speaker and a Protestant, originally from the Dunfanaghy area who married Charles Gallagher (1820-1905), an upwardly mobile Catholic shopkeeper. Since this woman was almost certainly English-dominant, perhaps knowing little Irish, it is safe to speculate that this exerted a huge influence on the language of the household.

Despite these Anglicising trends, a microcosm of the national pattern, Irish did not die out as a vernacular in the household or in the area, as might have been expected. Coláiste Uladh and its visitors, professional well-to-do people from urban areas; scholars and academics, including Pearse, Casement, Agnes Farrelly, Henry Morris, J.L. Lloyd and others, succeeded in giving Irish a new esteem, in some ways rivalling that of English, a position which it had not enjoyed for at least three centuries. The fact that Irish now had some kind of economic advantage was of central importance to this readjustment in the local attitude. Although that generation of my ancestors preferred English for sound reasons, they deliberately chose not to let Irish go as it had become advantageous to know it, both from a pragmatic economic viewpoint, and because it also earned them extra social prestige in front of the urban summer visitors who came yearly to learn the language.

A detailed study would shed light on the impression I have that my grandmother's generation were generally more bilingual than the generation that came immediately after them. They experienced the change from English-medium instruction with very little Irish being taught at all, to the bilingual programme, introduced in 1904. After the establishment of the Free State, Irish became the sole medium of instruction in Gaeltacht schools and in a great many others also, so that opportunities to hear and practise English actually became more limited. Many of those raised in the forties and early fifties have remarked on the difficulties they faced when they first went abroad to Scotland, as most of that generation were invariably forced to do. One member of the community, who was adopted, told me that although he had arrived at seven years of age in Donegal knowing no Irish, he changed in the course of seven years to being a dominant Irish-speaker, forgetting most of the spoken English he knew. Like many others, this caused him some hardship and embarrassment when he emigrated, since he was by then unable to express himself easily in English for any practical purpose. Many people of that generation testify that they had no practical command of English when they went away to work, which made an already traumatic experience more difficult for them. This led some to introduce English as a family language when they had children of their own to spare their own offspring the traumas they had suffered.

Ironically, my mother was Irish-dominant until she went to St Louis' Convent in Monaghan for her secondary education, at that time a privilege that was unfortunately and unjustly denied to most of her primary school mates. Although this was an 'A' school in which all subjects were taught through the medium of Irish, it was here that she became really fluent in English, as the majority of pupils were from English-speaking homes. She retained her Irish, however, and continued to use it. In our family in Gortahork, a pattern of relatively balanced bilingualism developed. My father (originally from Macroom) and mother spoke English together and my mother spoke Irish to us. My father encouraged us to speak Irish at all times, often stating that he wished he could speak it as easily as we could, thereby impressing upon us the value of our bilingualism.

Irish is, then, one of my two first languages. I think of it as my maternal language and of English as my paternal language, which reflects the pattern of use in the household where I grew up. I cannot remember a time when I did not know both languages. Indeed, there must have been a time when I did not realise that my immediate environment was a bilingual one. However, I discovered the difference early on in life. One story about my early years, repeated so often that it now seems like memory, relates that I once ran out in front of an oncoming car, from which I had a narrow escape. The driver braked, got out of his car and began loudly to scold me, probably because he himself had got a bad fright. He was using English. I piped up that I 'had' no English (*'Níl Béarla ar bith agam!'*) whereupon he immediately switched to Irish. I then retorted in Irish, that I 'had' no Irish either. (*'Níl Gaeilge ar bith agam ach oiread!'*)

In a way, this story epitomises the way the languages interacted with one another during my youth and the way that they still do. There was television (I had arrived about five months before RTÉ), with the Vietnam War, *Daithí Lacha*, *Wanderly Wagon* and both Charles Mitchell and Don Cockburn reading the *Nuacht* in Irish as well as the *News* in English. There was the bilingual situation at home and there was school – Caiseal na gCorr, a small three-teacher school where the great majority of pupils came from Irish-speaking homes with two Irish-speaking parents, and who were consequently Irish-dominant. Perhaps their knowledge of English in the infant classes was less than I understood at the time. We never spoke English except during English class – one hour a day, but I don't remember anyone having any problems with the language. Children of returning emigrants would join the class periodically, but seemed to become active speakers of Irish very quickly.

I remember that a similar situation obtained in one family of our neighbours in Gortahork, whose mother was not from

Donegal, but who, as I recall, could make a fair fist of Irish when necessary. Although she herself was English-dominant, her children, our playmates, all spoke Irish well. In our play, we used Irish mostly among ourselves with no sense that we were doing anything extraordinary. Indeed, those members of that family who still live locally are very active in the community and committed Irish-speakers, largely, I would venture, because of their early exposure to two languages and their complementary worlds. In another family, neither of the parents were from the area or had any connection with it. One of the children from that house has gone on to become one of the most admired and successful Irish-language broadcasters in the region.

I think I began to develop a keener sense of my own bilingualism when I was about eight or nine. I have always been an avid reader and, at that time, read mostly in English. English books were more readily available and often Irish books were not aimed at a young readership. There was also the problem of having books written by authors using Irish that differed from the variety we used daily. I found myself one day thinking about something and realised that I was using English for thinking. Gradually, I began to understand that usage could lead to one language dominating the other and I became concerned that perhaps my Irish would be adversely affected. It wasn't that I tried to stop thinking in English, but more the case that I realised that I'd have to make more of an effort to balance my use of English with an equal usage of Irish. This was the beginning of the development of the consciousness that I hold to this day towards Irish language and culture. It encompasses the idea that Irish is embattled and threatened by the great and alluring power of its stronger counterpart, English. It includes the idea that all those who support the language, or work for it, and who speak it mainly when they can, actually make a positive difference as far as Irish is concerned.

Such an epiphany would not appear to be so unusual. I was struck, on a visit to Hawai'i a number of years ago, that two prominent members of the language revitalisation movement whom I met there had similar narratives to tell. Both related how, as English-dominant children, with only a halting knowledge of the Hawaiian language, they had begged their older fluent relatives to begin speaking Hawaiian to them, so that they could become fluent. This action on their part directly led to their active involvement in trying to stem the language decline they witnessed daily around them in their youth.

The condition of being endangered inevitably generates a certain obsession with the future vitality of the language. My obsession originated during that period of my life, when my awareness of the fragility of the future of a language that I used regularly became gradually more sensitised. For me, from then on, Irish could no longer be taken for granted, but must be nurtured and protected and encouraged.

Looking back to the linguistic situation at home, it might have been much easier for my mother not to bother with Irish in the house at all and raise us all with English first – thinking that we'd get Irish at school. But she realised, correctly I think, that if Irish were to be a really meaningful part of our lives, it would also have to be a part of our home life. Furthermore, my parents ran a hotel and a small farm so that we were in regular contact with many local people who worked in the business and on the land. Irish was the usual language for most of them. They included many wonderful people who indulged us greatly as children. One of them, Róise McAuley, our regular minder for many years, was a particularly outstanding individual. From Droim na Searrach, near Gortahork, she was witty, humorous and one of the kindest and most affectionate people I was ever lucky enough to know well. Significantly, she was also Irish-dominant and although she spoke English functionally, she really flourished when she used Irish. We could never have used English with her and never did. Even today, certain words and expressions bring her to mind when I hear them or think of them. In describing this period of my life, I realise I am giving a somewhat idyllic picture. This is not really my intention. My point is rather to highlight the ordinariness of the bilingual situation for us as children at the time.

So Irish was a constant and natural presence which caused us no difficulty. Of course, as siblings we also sometimes used English, usually when playing with other children, but my mother had a particularly effective way of putting a stop to that if she considered it was going too far. She would call out chidingly, *'Cá bhfuil na Sasanaigh bheaga?'* (Where are the little English people?), or words to that effect, making us somewhat ashamed to be speaking English. She had inherited her linguistic consciousness from her father, a native of Kilcar in south Donegal, where the dominant vernacular changed from Irish to English during his lifetime.

I began to read seriously in Irish in my last years in Caiseal na gCorr, which had a relatively good library containing quite a number of Irish books. *Gasúr de chuid Bhaile na nGrág* by the Rosses writer Tadhg Ó Rabhartaigh was actually a part of the curriculum. This book was written in the old script, which was difficult at first, since we had been taught only the *cló rómhánach*, but I remain grateful that I had such an early introduction to the *cló gaelach*. *Dealg Eochaidh* and *Na Rianaigh Abú*, both by the gifted writer Seán Ó Mulláin, great swashbuckling stories of the Ó Riain family in seventeenth- or eighteenth-century Ireland, were some other books I read during these years.

At secondary school in Falcarragh I met other students that were previously known only by sight or by hearsay, but because they were from the three other national schools on our side of the parish, Irish was our language from the start. Although some teachers, notably those in history and geography and in mathematics, through personal commitment, made valiant attempts at teaching through Irish, school policy may be charitably described as somewhat *laissez-faire* and English became the language of instruction by default for the majority of subjects. It was a new school, the result of an amalgamation of three previously-existing academies. No proper provision was ever made to ensure that Irish-medium instruction would become a part of the school ethos, despite the participation of many who would have regarded themselves as pro-Irish in the negotiations and planning. Consequently, by the end of our third year we were being taught everything but Irish through English, though we still used Irish to communicate amongst ourselves and with our teachers who were Irish-speakers. Many of us became involved in debating and public speaking through the Gael-Linn leagues for secondary schools with some of our teams reaching the All-Ireland finals and one year winning the competition.

I progressed to Galway with a number of school companions in 1979 to study for a BA. Irish was by then one of my main interests. UCG was something of a revelation for me, since, because of a deliberate policy in the university promoting the use of Irish in everyday college life, the language could be heard in casual use in a wide range of contexts. To some extent, Irish had been a familiar vernacular that I used with others I knew, but it would have been unusual for any of us to use it with strangers, without first checking whether they spoke it. To that extent, we were frequently shy in our use of it with others. In my Irish class there were people from different parts of the West, mainly from coastal Conamara, but also from the inland mountain country around Loch na Fuaidh and another from Ceathrú Thaidhg in North-West Mayo. We also had one from Kerry. There were also excellent Irish-speakers from urban Galway, from Dublin and from Clare. I noticed that I frequently heard Irish being used by porters, librarians and other staff members during their work. Many lecturers who were not in the Irish department used Irish regularly. It was a very positive and affirmative experience. The realisation that Irish had the potential to be more than just for the domestic and familiar grew stronger, particularly during my postgraduate studies for an MA in Irish. My confidence in the public use of the language began to develop side by side with my deepening awareness of the cultural and literary heritage of Irish and its significance as a vital element in Irish life.

I had always been interested in Scottish Gaelic, having been deeply impressed with the renowned play *The Cheviot, the Stag and the Black, Black Oil*, about the Highland Clearances, produced by the Scottish theatre company Seven Eighty Four and broadcast on BBC (we could get a decent BBC reception from an aerial erected on a nearby hillside). There had also been a live link between BBC Radio Scotland and Raidió na Gaeltachta called *Ciamar a tha sibh?* We were incredibly fortunate that during successive years, two very committed and enthusiastic graduates of the University of Edinburgh, Mark Wringe and Alan Esslemont, came to Galway as Scottish Gaelic teaching assistants. They taught Scottish Gaelic, not merely by reading texts, but as a spoken foreign language – from the beginning, making us pronounce the words with the unique pronunciation of Scotland until we could say them and finally utter complete sentences in the language. They also warned us of the 'false friends', words recognisable to us from their Irish counterparts, but carrying different meanings. Of course, knowing Irish well was a tremendous advantage and we learned quickly. Additionally, they both imbued us with a unique perspective on Scottish Gaelic history, folklore, music, song and literature. From them, we learned about the dire state of the Gaelic language in Scotland in the mid-1980s, having almost no status in public life. Children from Gaelic-speaking homes were taught through mostly the medium of English, apart from some instruction in Gaelic, and the number of speakers in the younger age cohorts was in serious decline. Even at university level, the language of instruction for those taking Scottish Gaelic was predominantly English, although there had been some attempts to redress the situation. They often remarked how pleasantly surprised they were when they heard RTÉ radio announcers turn easily to Irish to make an announcement about Irish programming. Such a thing would have been unheard of in Scotland. They themselves were involved in the first attempts to address the disastrous neglect of Gaelic as a vernacular, a movement which has had many successes since then.

The language philosophy of Máirtín Ó Cadhain, particularly as outlined in *Páipéir Bhána agus Páipéir Bhreaca*, became important to me at this time. In reading Ó Cadhain's work, I became convinced that his advocacy of confrontation as a means to achieve equality for Irish was the best way to progress. I slipped into what Seamus Heaney has called 'binary thinking', believing that English had dispossessed Irish and that it must be rejected if Irish was to flourish again. Given the polarity of language debates in Ireland, and the kind of cultural environment at university, this was a fairly predictable viewpoint. It was my vantage on language issues for many years, and I agreed with others who held this view.

An organisation influenced by Ó Cadhain's thought, Cearta Gael in Donegal in the 1970s and 1980s, wished to expose what they thought were deliberate policies of neglect towards Irish in a number of areas in public life. They were idealists who had deliberately moved to the Donegal Gaeltacht to raise families in an Irish-speaking environment. They spoke excellent Irish and were fully committed intellectually and emotionally to the defence of the language. Using what became an increasingly confrontational approach, in line with Ó Cadhain's ideas, they tried to implement change and to strengthen language policy in education, in the courts and in the church at a local level. Ó Cadhain himself had engaged in similar confrontations in his native Galway Gaeltacht. Although he never enjoyed mass support there, his great personal charisma and his status as a local hero ensured that he had a loyal following, who were later to become influential activists on behalf of Irish themselves. However, in the case of Cearta Gael, their adversarial tactics eventually alienated many people, who began to oppose and boycott them actively. Their 'outsider' status prevented them from retaining a firm local following, although some certainly shared their concern about the failure of professionals charged with the maintenance of the language to do their utmost on its behalf. The campaign became entrenched and stalemated and no practical progress was made. This movement was important in Donegal in bringing the issue of language protection and planning into public discussion at a local level. It initiated healthy debate about the position of the language in a Gaeltacht area and what that would and should be. In a recent Raidió na Gaeltachta programme, a number of those who had been engaged in the events all agreed that the position of Irish as a vernacular was much weaker now, particularly among young people, than it had been in the late seventies when the campaign was at its height. Unfortunately, it also seemed that the bitterness engendered during that period was still exercising a negative effect on any cooperative attempts to redress the situation. At that time, influenced by Ó Cadhain's ideas, upon which many of their precepts were founded, I fully agreed with both the principles and the strategy of Cearta Gael, although I was never involved in the campaign. In recent years, I have come to revise my views, considering the polarisation which arose from these events ultimately damaging. The implementation of a new Language Act, however limited its scope, provides the possibility for a new departure, and an opportunity for cooperation toward common aims, despite real differences of opinion on issues of language. It is to be hoped that all those involved will seize this chance, since the maintenance of Irish needs all the help it can get at the moment.

Minister Éamon Ó Cuív's espousal of the Language Rights Bill in the 1990s, and his organisation of public meetings to consult with Irish-speaking communities as to what their needs were, provided a much-needed impetus in highlighting the link between the language issue and a broader cultural and economic programme. Those who put this matter on the agenda of the local community are also to be commended. The Bill currently being implemented is important in that it rightly puts the onus on the machinery of the state to adopt positive, affirmative action policies in regard to the Irish language. Despite over eighty years of self-government, and a constitution in which the Irish language enjoys primary status, state bureaucracy has constantly and in some cases deliberately neglected its duty to protect and encourage the use of the Irish language in its heartlands. In fact, the state has been one of the strongest forces of Anglicisation in Irish-speaking regions because of a great disparity between its official rhetoric and its day-to-day functioning. This may be difficult to believe, given the subsidies that the state also provides for Irish-speaking areas, and some change in this regard has been evident in recent years. It should be remembered, however, that these subsidies are dispensed through a punitively-oriented system, which tries to catch people out rather than to support and encourage them. In general, state employees, doctors, nurses, social workers, social welfare officials, *gardaí* and even sometimes teachers have not been practically required to be Irish-speakers, despite official policies. When they were competent in the language, it usually happened by default. Such a *de facto* English-only policy of officialdom toward the Irish language transmits a subliminal message, suggesting that, despite its eminent position in the constitution, *Irish is not that important really*, and people are reminded of this every time they have to deal with state officials. Those whose children require speech therapy, or who have monoglot children under school age dealing with hospital officials, provide stark examples of the need that exists but that has not been satisfactorily met. Frequently, the response is to discourage parents to use Irish in favour of English. Nurses try to have 'Gráinnes' changed into 'Graces' on their birth certificates. There are no crèche facilities for Irish-speaking families outside the Gaeltacht – 'Sure, isn't it far easier to speak English!' This is to be the subliminal message and it undermines an accepted positive attitude to language among its speakers, making their vernacular a social and political issue that is a source of discomfort for many. Since language is intimately linked with individuals' sense of self and their interconnected linkages with community, such encounters chip away at positive identification with the language and can be only regarded as debilitating and degrading assaults.

I have tried to show through relating my own experience of bilingualism in this short essay that Irish can flourish positively in a hospitable environment as it did during my own socialisation process. During that time we were often told that Irish was 'no load to carry'. My early realisation of Irish's endangered status led me to a career in teaching and promoting the language in various ways. The account is perhaps useful in that it provides another portrayal of a personal experience of the Irish language. Hugo Hamilton's recent excellent memoir, *A Speckled People*, gives a view of the struggle his father engaged in to bring him up in a bilingual German- and Irish-speaking household where English was forbidden. It has been reviewed as a damning critique of the futile practice of trying to raise children in a language that is not a community vernacular, but I believe the book is more subtle than that. Notions of compulsion, coercion, intimidation and inflexibility are issues which are cogently and thought-provokingly addressed in the book. One thing that clearly emerges is the sense of embattlement that Hamilton's father felt regarding the Irish language and the rhetoric he used to defend his position. Hamilton is right in criticising such ideology. Hamilton speaks of the term *breac* or 'speckled' as being a mark of impurity and of fragmentation, the contention being that those who were unable to speak Irish were less than fully Irish. This is the same word that is used in the term *breac-Ghaeltacht*. It almost has connotations of fever and disease. However, the term *breac* also has positive associations, which like older meanings of the word Gaeltacht we are bound to examine and embrace. People can be *chomh folláin le breac*, 'as healthy as a trout', and eat *bairín breac*, the rich fruit bread closely associated with Hallowe'en and with prophecy. The world we live in today is a speckled world and we must realise that we are all *breacdhaoine*, 'speckled people'. We can only gain by embracing such a concept.

The time for ideological enforcement may be coming to an end. But this must be true for 'English only' also. Those who wish to, wherever they dwell, have the right to expect support for their choice to bring up Irish-speaking children in an enlightened and loving atmosphere devoid of fear and intimidation. Gaelscoileanna, TG4 and other developments have brought such a possibility closer to us, although we still have a long way to go. The Acadamh na Gaeilge initiative undertaken by UCG to provide university-level education through the medium of Irish is a very welcome new development.

The reluctance of the Government to push for official status for Irish in the EU demonstrates the deep entrenched ambivalence that still characterises the attitudes of many towards the language. It is an apathy that all Irish speakers realise we can ill afford.

At the moment, Irish belongs to a group of perhaps 3,000 languages on earth which are regarded as endangered. Many of these languages are spoken by no more than a few old people in communities where they functioned until relatively recently as the ordinary vernacular, intimately entwined with the social and cultural life of the community. These languages are seldom spoken nowadays except to scholars who are interested in recording them while they still may. The global phenomenon of language attrition is regarded by many as the loss of an irreplaceable part of the human diversity of the planet. Despite its inadequate policies concerning its oldest vernacular, Ireland has been at the forefront of language protection and development in a global context. Excluding the exceptional case of Israel, no other state has managed to protect and foster a threatened language as Ireland has done. The *Irish Times* columnist Kevin Myers has consistently likened the revitalisation project, and TG4 in particular, established in 1996, to DeLorean Motors, but his metaphor is a poor one, despite superficial similarities. DeLorean Motors was a pet project for one industrialist, which squandered state-sponsored funding as much as it did the planet's non-renewable resources. The project of creating a safe environment for Irish, on the other hand, despite its admissible inadequacies, is an attempt at trying to ensure the continuity of one strand of the planet's and this island's unique cultural richness, to which a significant number of Irish people, and increasing numbers of enthusiasts for the language worldwide remain committed. It may justifiably be likened more suitably to projects defending traditional, indigenous cultures and resources on a global scale.

There are those who would argue cogently that the rain forest and its inhabitants are merely in the way of progress and that the sooner they're gone the better, since it is too costly to protect them. They would probably say the same about the dwindling boglands. But the view that the rain forest should be protected is not invalidated by such opinion. Perhaps it is even strengthened. Today the California condor, a huge bird of prey with a massive wing span is in danger of extinction. A dedicated program has been instituted to breed condors for reintroduction to the wild. Devoted volunteers spend many hours documenting and tracking these magnificent birds, which are profoundly ill-suited to the intrusions of urban living. Many condors succumb to poachers, poison, swallowing indigestible materials and to other perils emanating from human encroachment on their natural habitat. Their maintenance and restoration is a precarious attempt, hanging in the balance, and one that may ultimately prove fruitless. But enough people believe in it and are committed to it as a worthwhile goal, a 'good thing'. Many other species throughout the world are being maintained, protected and fostered in an attempt to ensure that they will not be wiped off the face of the planet. The analogy between such protection programmes and that of the Irish language is clear; since the survival of these unique elements of global biodiversity can be justified, surely a salient part of human cultural diversity, made in Ireland by nameless generations, can also be defended. In protecting and fostering Irish and its culture we are also doing a 'good thing'. We need to learn how to do it better; to improve teaching; to realise that teaching alone is not enough to build bilingual communities; to shed our myopic monolithic attachment to 'English only' together with our fear and suspicion of the Irish other. It is then that we may truly begin to exist as a *post*-colonial entity.

Beetles With No Legs Are Deaf!

Muireann Ní Mhóráin

Aithníonn ciaróg ciaróg eile. The title above refers to a joke which was popular at one stage with my family. I was reminded of this joke in the child development clinic one day when one of my children was having a routine aural comprehension test. The nurse was visibly appalled when I told her that the two-year old was being raised through Irish. She started telling me that it would certainly confuse him, cause speech delay and learning difficulties. I said nothing to contradict her unfounded opinion but courteously asked that she would speak to him in Irish.

She looked at him and he at her. With obvious irritation she said to him *'Dún an doras!'* The child looked from *an doras* to *an bhanaltra* to *mamaí* but did not move towards *an doras*. The nurse sighed impatiently and repeated the order *'Dún an doras!'* and the child did not respond. The lecture was delivered with obvious glee. My child's lack of understanding of language was caused by poor parenting owing to the infliction upon him of two languages. On and on she went and the child, trying to get her attention, was ignored. Suddenly he shouted 'The door *is* closed!'

Was the nurse impressed with his comprehension skills? Did she note his ability at the age of two to translate from one language to another? Did she praise him for his ability to express himself in a second language? No, but she did suggest speech therapy might be advisable. Neither mother nor child returned to the clinic. The beetle will also wait.

Muireann is ainm dom. There are many strange customs in Ireland and a particularly peculiar one is to respond to Irish names with the question 'What's that in English?' I was recently listening to an RTÉ news item about a dolphin in the Shannon estuary. The RTÉ newsreader informed listeners: 'The dolphin's name is Feichín which in English is Fergus.' Apart from the fact that the name Fergus and Feichín have nothing to do with each other, why would anyone share such information with us? How would people react if RTÉ started telling us that Kofi Annan, whose real name is Kevin Noone, made a statement today. Or how about asking the Italian Prime Minister, when he arrives to Dublin Airport during Ireland's presidency of the European Union, if Silvio Berlusconi *really is* his name?

An síneadh fada, the accent in Irish, is found on a keyboard by holding down the *Ctrl* button and the *Alt* button when pressing a vowel. This is not a difficult action. It does not require any advanced knowledge of technology to execute but amazingly all workers in financial institutions and all medical administrators seem to have a specific learning disability in this area. They all suffer from *síneadh fada-exia* which renders them unable to put a *fada* on vowels. A common symptom of the disorder is to blame the computer.

By strange coincidence some of the same people also suffer from an inability to apply basic rules of the alphabet to the Irish language and can never figure out where a surname such as *Ní Mhóráin* should be placed in a list of names. The same symptom as above is often evident, i.e. blaming the computer. This is particularly strange when one remembers that there is an 'O' in a huge number of Irish surnames and computers and telephone directories seem to be able to deal with them without bother.

So where does this leave the child with the Irish surname? The stock dialogue frquently goes something like this:

> *'What's your name?'*
> *'Míde Ní Chonchubhair.'*
> *'What's that in English?'*

'There is no English for it.'
'How do you spell it?'
'M ... Í ... D...'
'Can't find it on the computer. It must be under some other name.'
'How could it be under another name?'
'The computer doesn't do Irish names. Are you sure that's your name?'
'Of course I'm sure that's my name.'
'Would it be under another name?'

On and on it goes ...

Ag siopadóireacht le mamaí. Off we go shopping. Speaking Irish to children in supermarkets gets all or any of the following three reactions:

Reaction 1
Some people, other children especially, stop in their tracks and stare open-mouthed at the Irish-speaking aliens. Staring back is the only deterrent.

Reaction 2
A smiling adult comes over and says sympathetically in hushed tones: 'Aren't you great, speaking Irish to them?', as if I were a Good Samaritan doing some linguistic act of mercy. Moving along swiftly is the best course of action.

Reaction 3
Not-so-smiley adult comes over (especially when gridlocked in check-out queue) and shares in graphic detail his/her own bad experiences of learning Irish when corporal punishment was not yet outlawed in our schools. Horrified children may be distracted by drawing their attention to the sweet display.

Ag dul ar scoil. The first of the *gaelscoileanna* were set up half a century ago primarily to provide education through Irish for those whose first language was Irish. At a time when the language was neither fashionable nor popular these schools struggled from year to year, gaining respect through their achievements. In the past 20 years the *gaelscoileanna* movement has flourished and there are now 150 *gaelscoileanna* outside the Gaeltacht and the vast majority of their pupils have no Irish support mechanism at home. Whilst the growth in the number of *gaelscoileanna* is in itself a most welcome development, children whose first language is Irish are, quite naturally, being swamped by the English-language enviroment and by English-speaking children and adults around them. The educational needs of the Irish-speakers (development of English, for example) are ignored. There is no curriculum set down for Irish or English for those children whose first language is Irish or for bilingual pupils.

As those who have no Irish begin their immersion in Irish, the complicated process of language-learning begins. The children hear the language constantly and begin to comprehend the language. They learn words (rather than phrases or sentences) and begin to speak the language. An interesting phenomenon of the language development is that the children's first attempts at communication through Irish are usually English spoken through Irish, that is to say, Irish words spoken in English word-order and where a verb is not known in Irish, the English being used with the suffix '*-áil*' tagged on at the end. '*Puttáil mé ar mo chóta*'. '*An féidir mé faigh briosca?*'

The fact that very young children with no Irish can develop such intricate language skills through immersion is fantastic for them, but can be disastrous for the Irish-speakers who do not recognise the Irish of their peers as the language spoken at home but rather as a new (third) language to be learned and spoken by them in school. As time goes by and more waking hours are spent in school, the school Irish takes over and the Irish-speakers use their 'home Irish' less and less. The bilingual child becomes trilingual with English becoming the dominant language and their '*Gaelscoilis*' in second place.

Children in our schools who have learning difficulties or learning disabilities are referred to psychologists for assessment.

They are tested by means of standardised diagnostic tests. Recommendations are made and, if appropriate, extra resources are allocated based on the assessment results. Children whose first language is Irish are tested by use of the same tests as there are no standardised diagnostic tests available in Irish. Children who have no learning difficulties can score very poorly in these tests due to lack of comprehension of the tests. Their reading scores ignore the fact that Irish reading is introduced before English reading in many Gaeltacht schools and in many *gaelscoileanna*. Children with severe learning disabilities can be misdiagnosed because of the absence of tests in Irish.

The results of a study of the teaching of maths in primary schools carried out some years ago initially suggested that children learning maths through Irish were behind their peers in English-medium schools. Further investigation revealed that all children were tested through English and the Gaeltacht/*gaelscoil* children did not understand the test vocabulary. When the testing was carried out through Irish the results were reversed! I wonder what reaction would follow if the Department of Education and Science were to announce that children in our schools would be assessed through French from now on.

But all is not lost. My children's rights are to be defended by the soon-to-be-appointed Children's Ombudsman. This person 'will really listen to children and will work and engage positively with them at their level… will promote the rights of all children… will be committed to putting the needs of children first' according to the recently-published job advertisement, but it is not necessary for this 'champion for children and young people' to have any knowledge of Irish. So if my children or any other children whose first language is Irish wish to have 'their rights and welfare protected and promoted' they will have to do so in their second language regardless of their rights as citizens in a state where the first official language is Irish. I jest not!

And back to the beetle. A man trained a beetle to follow orders. When the beetle was told 'Forward march!', he did so.

When the beetle was told 'Right turn!', he did so. When the beetle was told 'Left turn', he did so. When he was told 'Halt!', he did so.

The man then pulled out each of the beetle's legs. He repeated all the orders but the beetle failed to respond. The man announced, 'This is proof of my theory. Beetles with no legs are deaf!'

I'll leave you to work out if you think there is any connection between the man's attitude to the beetle and many Irish people's attitude to the Irish language.

'Why Would Anyone Write in Irish?'

Éilís Ní Dhuibhne

The question in the title of this essay was put to me recently in all good faith by a professor of Anglo-Irish literature. English is not her first language and she was aware that her latest book, an outstanding study of an aspect of Anglo-Irish literature, had not received the attention it deserved internationally because it was written in her first language, Italian. She plans to write her next work in English.

That the possession of English as a mother tongue is a gift from the gods is not in doubt. English is the language of business, of the internet, and of the media. It is the international language of culture and literature, and increasingly it is the language of scholarship. To be born into an English-speaking country is to be born with a silver spoon in one's mouth. To write in English naturally confers on a writer the advantage of a potential readership numbering tens of millions and access to the international academic market. If James Joyce had written in Swedish or Danish or Dutch, would his works have found the international acclaim which has been their honour or good fortune to achieve? If he had written even in German or French or Italian, would he be in the position of having the longest list of scholarly articles, by far, of any Irish writer in the bibliography of the Modern Languages Association? And if *Ulysses* and *Finnegans Wake* had been written in Irish, what would the status of their author be today? Instead of being an international bestseller almost seventy years after his death, with an academic industry which thrives on exploring the most subtle nuances of his words, a library world which will pay many millions of euro for a few pages in his illegible hand, he would probably be a name known to a handful of Irish-speakers attending a winter school in the depths of County Mayo.

Every Irish writer now alive can speak, read and write in English. Some of those who write in Irish have English as their first language – among them the most well-known writers, such as Nuala Ní Dhomhnaill, Liam Ó Muirthile, and many others. In theory such writers could write in English, one might imagine. In Ireland, there is no practical necessity for writing in Irish, since everyone in Ireland can read English perfectly well. If one leaves aside the small and essential incentives offered by Bord na Leabhar Gaeilge in the way of grants, or the Oireachtas prizes, the practical advantages of choosing this language as the medium for poetry or fiction are nil. Irish-language writers rarely achieve international acclaim (it is true that *Cré na Cille* has been translated to Norwegian and Danish, but that is not international acclaim in the sense that the Joyce industry understands it). Indeed, even the best of them never really achieve national acclaim. No matter how excellent their work, no matter how successful they are within the Irish-language circles, they remain largely invisible in Ireland and the rest of the world. So why would anyone write in Irish?

In the case of those for whom Irish is their first language, the motivation is obvious. Among such writers are those born in the Gaeltacht and others who, although living in English-speaking places, were brought up with the language. There is an argument that it is imposssible to write well in any language other than one's first language, one's mother tongue. This, of course, is not true, as has been proven by Joseph Conrad and many bilingual Indian and North American writers. And it is certain that all Irish-language writers who were brought up speaking Irish in their homes, even in the Gaeltacht, are very proficient English-speakers as well. Nevertheless, the motivation for those who have Irish as their first language is obvious, even if it is not sensible in a worldly way.

Since the days of the Irish revival, a political motivation for writing in Irish has been a strong one – 'Ní tír gan teanga.' Patriotism, nationalism, the belief that Irish identity is defined ultimately by language and is dependent for its integrity on the Irish language, motivated the writers of the revival, and continued to provide a strong motivation for many writers ever since. I suspect that their numbers are dwindling, and, outside Northern Ireland, the political or nationalistic motivation for speaking or writing Irish is diluting constantly. Nevertheless it is still there. It is not my motivation for writing in Irish. There are two languages (at least) in Ireland, and personally I do not feel any less Irish when I speak or write in English than I do *as Gaeilge* (although I do feel different and will discuss this later). I do not believe however that the nationalism of the revival carries much weight these days with Irish-language writers. In addition, any sense of power which the language carried in the early days of the new state has long disappeared. Irish was once a key to success in certain areas of Irish life, but for many years it has been almost the opposite. One is in more danger of being a figure of fun nowadays if one is associated with Irish, than a figure of power and prestige.

An excellent reason for choosing Irish as a literary medium is an aesthetic reason. I feel there are writers, poets perhaps in particular (and Irish has in this century thrived much more in poetry than in prose), who elect Irish because they love its sounds, its cadences, its rhythms, the very music of the language. The work of art one produces in Irish is totally different from the one produced in English in the aesthetic sense. Prose too has a shape, a sound, a rhythm and a music, but it transcends linguistic boundaries much more easily than poetry does, since the meaning of a work of prose is at least of equal importance as its language or form. As far as poetry is concerned, form is more significant, and form carries meaning. To select Irish rather than English on aesthetic criteria is probably the purest, most artistic, most honest reason for saying 'Goodbye to English' and adopting Irish as one's literary medium.

But most people, writers included, are not pure, honest, and totally motivated by aesthetic considerations. I am not among that noble elite. So why, to answer my friend's question, would I write in Irish? There are, I am afraid, several reasons, quite a rag and bone shopful of them, and they are, I think, lurking where the ladders tend to start – in the heart, or in the deep-seated, elusive core of the personality. It is down there in the murky depths of the character and the heart that every novel, every poem, every picture, every piece of music, begins its journey to the surface of the earth where the artist who has mined it and pulled it up will hone it into a work of art. I am not sure what the psychological explanations of language are, but I would guess that the first language, the mother tongue, resides in the deepest part of the personality, second and subsequent languages perhaps somewhere closer to the surface, if one continues to use the archaeological metaphor.

English is my mother tongue, but my connections with the Irish language are intricate and deep-rooted, and they are intensely personal. My father was a native speaker, who was born and brought up in a Gaeltacht, Glenvar on Lough Swilly in County Donegal. He spoke a dialect of Irish which was rare then and is now almost extinct. My mother, however, did not speak Irish. My father was usually out of the house, pursuing the demanding life of a tradesman in the Ireland of the 1950s and 1960s (nine or ten hours' work a day, six days a week). Occasionally he had to travel away from home to other towns to find work, in the depressed Ireland of my youth, so English was the language of my home and of course the language of my surroundings – Ranelagh, in Dublin. Nevertheless I heard Irish, my father's strange esoteric Irish, from birth, and spoke to him in his own language.

When I was five I went to Scoil Bhríde in Earlsfort Terrace (now on Oakely Road in Ranelagh). This was an all-Irish school. It had been founded in 1917 by Louise Gavan Duffy, the French-born daughter of Sir Charles Gavan Duffy, founder of *The Nation*, and so had a tradition linking it to the Young Irelanders and the roots of modern Irish political and cultural nationalism. In those days the standard of Irish in Scoil Bhríde was high and we all spoke it fluently by the time we were six or seven. Some of the teachers came from Gaeltacht regions. Neither in Scoil Bhríde, nor subsequently in the Irish-speaking secondary school I attended, Scoil Chaitríona, did I ever encounter a teacher or anyone else who spoke Donegal Irish like my father. Indeed as soon as I set foot in school I discovered that even the prayers he had taught me in Irish employed not just a different accent but different phrases and words from those I had to chant with the other four-year-olds in Low Babies. *'Go mbeannaí duit, a Mhuire'* became *"Sé do bheatha, a Mhuire'* and so on. At the age of four I learned to deal with English, Donegal Irish, and the Irish of Earslfort Terrace – a mixture of Kerry and Conamara Irish, with the latter increasingly fashionable for some reason, presumably to do with the influence of Galway Irish on the official standard or *caigdeán oifigiúil*. There were no teachers from Cork (my personal favourite of all the dialects purely for its sounds) and nobody from Donegal or anywhere in Ulster. I do not know why, since many Donegal women trained as teachers. Perhaps they stayed at home or, if they emigrated, went to Scotland.

I understood from an early age that my father was a problematical entity in the world of school, which was part of the Irish-language community of Dublin. This was not only because he spoke Donegal Irish, the marginalised dialect, or came from Donegal, the place nobody from Dublin ever visited, it seemed, since it entailed a drive through Northern Ireland, which they wanted to recapture for the Republic but would prefer not to set foot or tyre in at the moment, *go raibh míle maith agat*, in case one of the natives would shoot them as they sped through in their Morris Minors. This was bad enough. But what was even worse was that my father was a real Gaeltacht man, a carpenter who spoke Irish because that is what his mother spoke, not because he was a member of Conradh na Gaeilge or a civil servant or an *aficionado* of the annual Oireachtas dinner-dance, like most of the other parents in Scoil Bhríde and Scoil Chaitríona. (I assume the other Gaeltacht people were either still in the Gaeltacht or else in Scotland, England, or America. They were certainly not in Ranelagh.) I sensed that nobody knew what to make of my father, that embarrassing phenomonen: the real thing. He was a quiet and very gentle person, like most Donegal men, but his Irish sounded primitive and barbaric, and it seemed to me that when he spoke it he, too, linked himself to something wild and savage. When he spoke his rare dialect he was a woodkern out of an engraving by Derricke; his navy overalls might as well have been a shaggy Irish cloak, distinguishing him dramatically from the mild-mannered civil servants, children of the revival, with their shabby tweed jackets, gold *fáinnes* and steely bicycle clips. There was no room for my father's Irish in the schools I attended or in the life I led as a child. I lost it.

All this was extremely interesting to the writer *in spe*, even if I was not conscious of it at the time. Change, liminality, loss itself, are always inspirational and are, perhaps, primary factors in the formation of the artist. My schools introduced me to the complexities of the Irish-language world and I understood very early that language is much more than a system of communication. I saw that it was layered, historically, geographically and socially, all of which I would have understood soon enough even if I had been an English monoglot. But bilingualism in Dublin ensured an early introduction to the political baggage of language. Irish-speakers felt special, felt more Irish than the other Irish, felt privileged in one sense and were happy members of a cosy club – indeed 'club' was a favourite word of theirs, Club an Chonartha, An Club

Leabhar. They were clubby and happy, on the one hand, and on the other were derided, criticised, and even hated. Hatred of the Irish language was an emotion one encountered more at that time than nowadays, although it still exists, and always shocks me when I come across it (how odd that a language and a culture should be vehemently hated – how philistine, how ignorant, how silly! And yet perfectly civilised, eductated, intelligent Irish people do hate it, sometimes). In the 1960s, the Language Freedom Movement, which was essentially an anti-Irish movement, sensibly opposed the idea of compulsory Irish in schools and state examinations, but less sensibly was simply and profoundly negative towards the very idea of Irish. As a pupil at an all-Irish school in Dublin, one learned that it was sometimes wise not to broadcast this fact too loudly. In short, being a bilingual child in Dublin in those days taught one to be ambivalent, to prevaricate, to negotiate at least two main cultures and several sub-cultures. It developed my social and cultural antennae, which was probably considerably more useful in the long run than chemistry or maths.

In a practical sense, the Irish schools taught me how to read, write and speak a servicable, neutral Irish. Although I have always spoken Ranelagh Irish, I could negotiate my way through all the dialects with ease from about the age of eight, long before Raidió na Gaeltachta finally enabled all the Irish-speakers of Ireland to find one another. My ear was attuned to many different dialects and social registers of both English and Irish. It was a splendid training for a writer.

There were flaws in this strange education. One major difficulty I recognise retrospectively was that although we took all our classes and examinations through Irish, we read very little in that language for pleasure. This was a major stumbling-block in a writer's development. I wonder if the most influential language on a young writer is the language he or she reads rather than the one they speak? That there is a close link between reading and creative writing is not in doubt. Somehow as a child in the linguistic context I have described I was an obsessive reader of books in English, but very seldom came across anything in Irish that seemed attractive; most of the time I did not come across anything at all. The only novel I remember reading with surprised pleasure was *Máire Nic Artáin*, a sentimental novel about a young Belfast woman. There seemed to be a total dearth of such fiction, the kind that would appeal to a girl reader. There was very little for children. *Reics Carlo*, the feisty detective of Harcourt Street, whom my husband and sons love even today, was not my cup of tea. I did not like the flimsy look of the books which were published in a penny-dreadful format, and I did not like whodunnits, and I did not like *Reics Carlo*.

The result of this neglect of reading in Irish was that, although I had made the decision to be a writer at a very early age, it never occurred to me to write in Irish. Everything indicated that the language of literature was English. All the books were in English, apart from a few text books. Everything I read was in English. Irish, the language of my education, seemed to exist in a non-literary world. People spoke it, taught in it, danced in it, went to clubs in it, but they didn't read it.

When I left school and went to college, University College Dublin, without hesitation I decided to study English, Pure English in fact. The thinking even of my teachers in Scoil Chaitríona was that a pupil who showed literary aptitude would study English, whereas Irish was for people who were linguistically inclined, or who were very patriotic, or who wanted to be teachers. If you wanted to be a writer, English was the subject for you.

Interestingly, however, Pure English, which consists of Modern, Old and Middle English, led me right back to where I had started from, back to Irish. This was partly as a result of my name, which was and is 'in Irish'. The Professor of Old English, Father Dunning, informed me when I was in second year that a Department of Irish Folklore had been established in the

College, and that the new professor was going to offer a course
to the Old and Middle English students on 'The Folktale and
Medieval Literature'. 'You will be interested in this,' he said,
'because your name is in Irish.' His was a somewhat simplistic
view of the world but it was functional. I was interested.

Strangely enough, I had no idea of what folklore was before I
began that course and entered the Department of Irish Folklore.
That there were thousands and thousands of stories collected and
stored in the manuscripts of that department was a revelation to
me, the lover of stories. I had selected Pure English with the lofty
ambition of penetrating to the roots of literature before setting off
on my own great odyssey as a writer. Now I discovered that the
roots of literature were not in *Beowulf* or *The Battle of Maldon*, or
indeed anything that had been written down, but that a still
deeper and older layer of narrative was to be found in oral
tradition. The archives of the Department of Irish Folklore, and
the whole world of the international folktale, to which I was
introduced in a brilliant, thorough, scholarly way by my now
husband Bo Almqvist, were to me like a new continent, a magical
world I had not known existed. And most of the texts, the stories,
were in Irish! So it seemed to me that this was where all the fiction
had been hiding, and where all the fiction had started. By a
circuitous path, I had found my way to it.

Still, when I began writing and publishing short stories at
about this time, I wrote in English, and continued to do so for
many, many years. During my years as a postgraduate student of
folklore I visited the Gaeltacht in Donegal on a number of
occasions, and collected stories and songs from Joe Mac
Eachmharcaigh in Gortahork. Later, I began to visit Dunquin in
Kerry very regularly, and became friendly with such wonderful
Irish-speakers as Joe Daly, Bab Feirtéar, Muiris and Seán Ó
Gaoithín, and others. Once or twice I wrote a poem in Irish
while in Dunquin, but it was not until Cliodhna Ní Anluain
invited me to workshop some stories with Amharclann de hÍde
in 1995 that I actually wrote a work in Irish – my first play, *Dún*

na mBan Trí Thine, which is based on a legend told in many places but which I had first heard in Dunquin.

The play, directed by the brilliant Kathy McArdle, was a success. I followed it with another play, *Milseog an tSamhraidh*, which was less successful although I believe it to be the better play. Later I wrote *Casadh an Taperecorder*, which won the Oireachtas prize of drama and was broadcast as a radio play by RTÉ in 2003. Caoilfhionn Nic Pháidín and Seán Ó Cearnaigh of Cois Life, a new Irish-language publishing house, published the first two plays, and Caoilfhionn then suggested to me that I write a popular novel in Irish. It seemed to be my fate to employ, when writing in Irish, genres I had not used in English. I had written neither plays nor popular novels in that language. However, during my summer in Dunquin in 2000, I, the hater of *Reics Carlo*, wrote a whodunnit, *Dúnmharú sa Daingean*, which also enjoyed great success and became an Irish-language best-seller. In 2003 I published a second and more serious novel, *Cailíní Beaga Ghleann na mBláth*. I have also written a short story in Irish, and will continue to write fiction in Irish.

Why do I do it? When *Dún na mBan Trí Thine* was staged in the Peacock Theatre, I discovered various things about writing in Irish. In the first place, I found the warm reception the play received from the Irish-language community in Dublin overwhelming. I had anticipated brickbats from the establishment, but instead I found that there was a great welcome for a new voice in the field. That was seductive in itself. I also realised that I shared a culture and frame of reference with the Irish-language community, which I had repressed in my literary work until then. Although I draw on Irish folklore when writing in English I think it is fair to say that it is proferred in small doses and of course translated to English. In Irish, I was able to assume a foreknowledge of many aspects of folklore and Irish literature in my audience, and the sense of writing within a tradition was strong. At the same time, my play was extremely experimental in form and it seemed to me that Irish-language audiences were more tolerant of experiment than the conventional audiences for English plays in Dublin.

Dún na mBan Trí Thine examines the life of a repressed artist, Lennie, and moves between Irish and English cultures, old and new Ireland, between tradition and modernity, between the supernatural and the real. Since I was four, I have been moving between different worlds, particularly between the world of my father, the Irish-speaking west of Ireland, the medieval past, and the modern urban world of Dublin. Much of my writing in general has explored this fascinating and complex territory, has examined the different sides of Ireland, and is a sort of description of what Ireland is, in all its variety. It is also an attempt by me as an artist to negotiate the boundaries of the different worlds. My work in Irish in particular has dealt with these issues. *Dúnmharú sa Daingean*, although it seems and is a light-hearted comedy, a parody almost of detective fiction, also examines or looks at (since I am a writer, not a social scientist) the modern Gaeltacht and modern Dublin. My character moves from one to the other. Similarly, in *Cailíní Beaga Ghleann na mBláth*, Máire, the heroine, moves from Dublin to an Irish college in Cork. The schoolchild world of Dublin, of *Gaeilgeoirí*, and of the relationship of Irish-speakers with the Big House, among other things, is dealt with in this novel. I have found it easier to deal with themes relating to Irish cultural and linguistic identity in Irish than in English, although I have written about these issues in my novel *The Dancers Dancing*, where Yeats' image of the dancer and the dance is used to convey the ultimate wholeness of the Irish linguistic and cultural experience, and where instead of viewing Irish and English as separate sides of Irish identity, the heroine, Orla, learns to view them as complementary and enriching.

I have not found it easy to embrace Irish as a literary language. As I write, I learn, and that has also been an incentive to continue. I have also been encouraged, however, by the knowledge that I have with some of my works found an audience, and I am not sure that I would continue to write in

Irish if I discovered that I was not being read or listened to at all, which is always a risk with every Irish-language publication. Promotion of Irish books is essential so that at least the main target audience will be aware of their existence – this is not always the case.

In conclusion, I would say that I write in Irish primarily for personal reasons: the Irish language is a part of my cultural background, and I am reluctant to say goodbye to it. I have found that my voice as an author is the same, however, when I write fiction, whether it be in English or in Irish, something which surprises me. When writing articles such as this, I detect a difference. This essay, for instance, was initially written in Irish, due to a mistake on my part. Since I had communicated only in Irish with the editor of the volume I had somehow assumed that I should write the essay in Irish. When I had to rectify the mistake by translating my own essay to English, I realised that it was written in a more colloquial, informal, friendly way than it would have been if originally composed in English. The fact is that when writing in Irish one feels that one is part of a group – the reality is that one is personally acquainted with many of those who are likely to read the text. In English, one is writing for a large anonymous audience, for an unknowable entity. This certainly affects one's attitude and tone, and may influence style itself. I have toned down the style of this piece in translating it but am aware that it is still more intimate and considerably more informal than it would have been had I written it in English from the outset. Although English is my main language, I feel at home, and relaxed, when I am writing in Irish. It was my father's language. It was the language of a large part of my childhood. Of course I feel at home there – and that is my reason for writing in it and continuing to do so. I imagine it is the most common reason among those who make this strange and silly choice, to write in Irish.

There is, though, as for many Irish-language writers, another reason, less personal, and more social. I was heartened above all not only by the good sales of my novel, *Dúnmharú sa Daingean*, but also by the admission of a woman friend in the Gaeltacht that it was the first novel in Irish she had enjoyed, or perhaps even read, in years. I remembered my brief encounter with *Máire Nic Artáin*. And I remembered a particular magic day in my childhood, when I was nine. I was on holidays in Glenvar, the Donegal Gaeltacht of my father's childhood. A friend gave me a copy of Louisa May Alcott's *Little Women*. I read this sentimental but immortal story of girls in Concord during the American Civil War while sitting in the deep window seat of an ancient thatched cottage looking out over a valley on the banks of Lough Swilly where my ancestors had lived for centuries, speaking Irish, and where Irish was still the daily language of most people. I stayed in the window until night fell and I had finished the book. It was a day of pure delight: the beautiful cottage, the summer's day, and the discovery of a great novel (for young people) which I would cherish for years.

A great novel in English. How wonderful it would be if a little bookworm girl with literary aspirations could experience that intense reading pleasure, which will seldom be as profound as it is when she is eight or nine years old, with a great novel written in Irish! If that could happen, there would be no need to ask the question, 'Why write in Irish?'

How I Discovered Irish
or How Irish Discovered Me

Gabriel Rosenstock

According to the best recent estimates, in the present century 2,500 languages are likely to be lost – which is what happens when the last living speakers turn to another language. A total of 2,500 languages in a hundred years is an average of one language every two weeks ...

Andrew Dalby, *Language in Danger* (2002)

One wakes up one morning to the realisation that one has written or translated about 120 books in Irish and edited twice that amount – too busy to count – and one asks, 'How did all this come about?' I am now in my fifties. Both of my parents have gone to the Pure Land. Now would be a good time to look back and see if there was any sense to it all.

Let's start with parents then, shall we? My mother was a Keane (Ó Catháin) from Greethill (Cnocán Íomhair), situated in the lush, lonely fields of Athenry. Her people had come down from the North in the mid-seventeenth century. Raftery was a frequent visitor to my mother's ancestral home and, though blind, he gave fulsome praise to the beauty of Úna Ní Chatháin and the welcome he always found in Greethill:

Tar éis na Nollag le cónamh Chríosta
Ní chodlód choíche má mhairim beo
Go dté mé siar go Cnocán Íomhair
Mar is áit bhreá shaoithiúil é nach dtiteann ceo ...

God, the terrible things that can happen in the space of a few generations! My mother had nothing but botched school-Irish. And yet her English was peppered with hundreds of mellifluous Irish words and phrases. In shock, or wonderment, she would exclaim *Ababúna!* This would become the name of a small publishing company I founded which would publish her moving memoirs, *Hello, is it All Over?*

She went off nursing in Jersey – to complete her Anglicisation! There she met my father who was a medical student in the *Wehrmacht* (the Germans had invaded the Channel Islands). After World War II, my parents settled in Kilfinane, in East Limerick. I went to school locally. I remember learning the famous Brahms Lullaby in Irish. The words and the idioms would be challenging to a Leaving Certificate student today if presented as an unseen text. I had no difficulty with it at all. The renowned linguist Noam Chomsky tells us that the capacity for language is all practically there anyway, that it's just a matter of teasing it out. So, I was lucky that my teacher, Sister Celsus, was a native speaker of Cork Irish. I only realised this many years later. No wonder I am convinced that primary teachers of Irish should be native speakers or have near-native ability in the language.

I was the first Rosenstock to be born in Ireland. There were Germans in County Limerick long before us, the Palatines. When the paterfamilias died, it was the custom to bury the Bible with him. Eventually, they ran out of Bibles and that was the end of the German language in County Limerick!

I was the third in the family. Groucho Marx used to go on a lot about being the third. Is it something special? I don't know. Freud doesn't interest me all that much. His *Gesammelte Werke* were in the sitting room, but all in German. Anyway, one day, this first-born in Ireland, being a bit of an anarchist, started marching noisily through the house, uttering strange mantras in a loud voice. I can hear my father saying, '*Mein Gott! Was ist los?*' My mother explained the commotion. 'Not only can he read his

Irish reader, he has it off by heart; he's now reciting it to the walls, to the stairs, to the fairies – to anything or anybody keen on listening.' Or something to that effect. Hmm! Nothing's changed much in fifty years.

My anarchic energy was so much to the fore it was decided to send me packing at the age of nine to Mount Sackville, a preparatory college, where my mother had a sister, a pious nun. I recall reading *Little Lord Fauntleroy*. No, I said in my own mind, I'm not going to be an upper-class twit. Or did I? I much preferred the spirit of the wild – Huck Finn, Hiawatha. (To this day, I have more than a passing interest in Native American poetry.)

I was a voracious and a precocious reader. English was exercising its charms on me and I read widely – and strangely. A second-hand bookshop in Limerick yielded unlikely treasures, the letters of William Cowper, sermons by a Scottish divine, Blair by name, if I rightly recall, and he knew well how to blare. Getting to Limerick, one passed Lough Gur. Nobody told me that the word *gor* meant 'hatching'. I had to wait over forty years for an Englishman, Michael Dames, in his *Mythic Ireland*, to explain that a whole cosmology was hatched there!

My brother Michael drowned in Glendalough. It was decided not to send me to Clongowes, where he had been, but to Gormanston. (Would I have been Anglicised had I gone to Clongowes?) A Father Juniper OFM lent me a few books, including one which contained photos of writers. I fell in love with a photo of Edna St Vincent Millay (1892-1950), feeling mixed emotions as I savoured her longings:

> *Oh think not I am faithful to a vow ...*
> *Faithless am I save to love's self alone,*
> *Were you not lovely I would leave you now*
> *After the feet of beauty fly my own ...*

So there I was, reading American sonnets. An unusual way of attempting to become an aesthete. I couldn't get enough of

Edna. Perhaps this presaged my life-long quest for the goddess? Anyway, thus intoxicated, I myself began to write in a sensuous vein until the authorities couldn't take it anymore. I was too young to be excommunicated. So they expelled me. Thence to cold Rockwell where the opportunities of becoming an aesthete were crippled by the fact that Chesterton and Belloc were the favoured authors in the library, my copy of George Moore's *Heloise and Abelard* was confiscated and the only boarder who was interested in talking philosophy, a certain Jean-Claude Volgo, was thrown into the lake by the cauliflower-eared brigade.

Finally I got the chance to play Antony in *Antony and Cleopatra*. More passion: 'Give me my robe, put on my crown, I have immortal longings in me, now no more the juice of Egypt's grape shall moist these lips ...'

English was taking hold of me, in spite of many sojourns in summer colleges where one learned such things as *'Gael mise, nach uasal san ... Gael im' chroí ... Gael im' mheon ...'* – a heady cocktail, perhaps even a dangerous one, but it was competing with a new band on the scene called The Beatles. It was in summer college that I met a living Irish poet, *An Gabha Gaelach* (the Gaelic Blacksmith). At a *céilí* one night I became his *reacaire* or 'reciter'. It didn't matter to me if some of the lads thought the role of a *reacaire* to be a bit effeminate. I was only trying to impress the ladies and, furthermore, I was physically and verbally well able to defend myself.

Did you ever hear the story about the *Gabha* and Seán Ó Ríordáin? Exchanging pleasantries as they met, the *Gabha* said, *'Is bráithre iad lucht aon cheirde.'* ('Those of the same trade are brothers'.) Ó Ríordáin's riposte? *'Ar ndóigh, ní gabha mise!'* ('Of course, I'm not a blacksmith!') Anecdotes can keep us alive when there's precious little else to live on. Indeed, anybody thinking of devoting his or her life to the 'cause' had better be thick-skinned.

A Mass in Irish, in Rockwell, was a rare thing. On the only such occasion that I can recall, the celebrant, Fr 'Puff' Mullins

(An tAthair Seosamh Ó Maoláin) had me in thrall: *'Is sibhse salann an tsaoil!'* ('Ye are the salt of the earth!') Those Irish sibilants flowed like salt from his mouth. And I fell to thinking on the rich inheritance of the English language, Shakespeare and, not least, the Bible. What were the historical reasons which deprived Irish of such resources? What other resources were left? Where were they? The educational system at the time wasn't designed to encourage such thinking or to provide satisfactory answers. Does it today? Let others answer that. Fr Mullins was a bit of a hero of mine mainly because he was an eccentric. He taught languages. He had three of us for German. Once we spent a good thir(s)ty minutes in his room as he launched into an Italian class, not realising we were the 'Germans'. He rewarded our forbearance with a few buns from the priests' refectory. These created a dryness in the mouth and we were forced to help ourselves to the altar wine on our way out.

After Rockwell I suddenly became alarmed that I might be metamorphosing into Little Lord Fauntleroy after all – 'I have to go to England to be a Lord'. I absconded to Ros Muc, following in the footsteps of Pearse, though less innocently, meeting people who, then, had little or no English. One fellow who didn't like the cut of my jib gave a roar at me in Maidhcó's pub: *'Foc siar agus na seacht bhfoc!'* I didn't take offence. I noticed the emphatic *seacht* and the effect it had on f-words. I was learning – fearing much of what I saw and heard, feeling estranged but sucked in nonetheless.

Dinneen, the sorcerer in Jesuit garb, came along at the right time: *drúichtín* – 'a light dew … a dewdrop … a species of whitish snail; a slug…' On May mornings girls discovered the colour of the hair of their future husbands from the shade of the colouring of the first *drúichtín* they found. Not so much the Hidden Ireland as the hidden poetry of every word; words coming and going like wraiths, words invoked and bidden to stay; words like ladies in waiting, beckoning, winking shyly, their moist lips half-open, an utterance impending, an utterance not heard on the streets, an uncommon speech, secret syllables that might open up an Aladdin's Cave.

Trips to my father's neck of the woods, Schleswig-Holstein, didn't cure this infatuation with Irish, this dizziness. I met a well-off farmer there who spoke Platt or Low German. He loved to listen to Italian opera. Irish, I thought, was a bit like Platt – it had become a peasant language, but without the opera, only a dying memory of Carolan, friend of Italian composers. Was everything economics, then? I didn't have an answer. I hadn't read Marx. The young generation in Schleswig-Holstein were listening to AFN, American Forces Network in Germany, blithely on their way to becoming *níos Meiriceánaí ná na Meiriceánaigh féin*. Well, enough of that, says I! Let's explore more of the Gaeltacht, while it's still there.

My reading was as eclectic as ever – anthropology, Oriental philosophies. I took Irish as one of my subjects in UCC. Gangs of us, wandering minstrels, would find ourselves in the bosom of the Corca Dhuibhne Gaeltacht, discovering ourselves, or so we thought, and getting lost in successive waves of sorrow and hilarity.

Back in UCC, the INNTI poets emerged and we are surfing the energy of those tsunamis ever since, in one way or another. Does that mean that the connection between myself and Raftery is an unbroken one? No, I can't say that. Give me Rumi any day before Raftery. Basho before Ó Bruadair. Having worked with Irish all of my adult life, as an assistant editor in An Gúm, as an editor with the now defunct newspaper *Anois*, as a broadcaster with such programmes as *Anois is Arís*, even on the stage of the Damer, performing Pinter and others in Irish – all this, and more, coupled with the fact that our home, today, is Irish-speaking, most of the time, does all this mean that Irish has soldered my identity, so to speak? Not really. In certain situations traces of Little Lord Fauntleroy unwittingly emerge. And there's also the No-Mind, a state of non-identity that 'I' cultivate through the discipline of haiku.

Irish and Irishness is not a happy argument to enter into at all. I would like to caution against it, in fact. It's nightmarish. Don't ask me why – I don't really know – but I am much more at home in Isaac Bashevis Singer's descriptions of Jewish Poland than I am in Ó Cadhain's Conamara. I'm not sure if I could live in the Gaeltacht, for instance, or be fully integrated in any Western society. I'm nowhere happier, indeed, than in Kerala, India.

So, what has it all meant? What does it signify, this passion for Irish, this commitment to its survival? For one thing, it suits the anarchist, the non-conformist in me. I like being different. It is not so much a question of liking being different, I feel different. Come to think of it, we're all different, all unique, and there is an empowerment in waking up to that simple fact alone. Had we an Ireland today that was 90 per cent Irish-speaking, I would probably join the other 10 per cent – whatever that might be, Anglo-Irish, Hiberno-French ... anything you wish to imagine. I like minorities. The world needs them more and more as we jostle towards consensus, towards homogeneousness. My son-in-law comes from Sibiu in Transylvania. Sibiu is also an old German enclave known as Hermanstadt. Funny old world. Let's keep it like that.

I am attracted to mysticism. Have you ever heard of the Baal Shem Tov? He and his grandson, the Rebbe Nachman, are the founders of the Hasidic movement. The Baal Shem Tov believed that the divine spark was in everything – even in sin, as the oil is in the olive. While I firmly believe in cultural distinctiveness, I look forward to the day when humanity can share a higher spiritual awareness of what we all have in common:

Ceistíonn Krishnamurphy na Deisceabail
'Cé mé,
dar libh?'
arsa Krishnamurphy lena dheisceabail.
Freagra níor tháinig go ceann i bhfad.

'Is tú an Baal Shem Tov,'
arsa duine acu.
'Ní mé,' arsa Krisnamurphy.
'Is é an Baal Shem Tov
an Baal Shem Tov.
Ní mise eisean
ná ní eisean mise ...
Ach, ar ndóigh, sa mhéid is gur aon dream amháin is ea sinn,
tusa agus mise
agus ruball na muice
is féidir a rá ex cathedra gur mise an Baal Shem Tov
agus gur eisean mise.'

[Krishnamurphy Questions the Disciples
'Who am I
do ye think?'
says Krishnamurphy to his disciples.
The answer was a long time coming.

'You are the Baal Shem Tov,'
one of them says.
'I am not,' says Krishnamurphy.
'The Baal Shem Tov
is the Baal Shem Tov.
I am not he
he is not me ...
But, of course, since we are all the one
you and I
and the pig's eye
it can be stated ex cathedra that I am the Baal Shem Tov
and he, naturally, is me.']

I think as a poet. I feel as a poet. Unapologetically so. Being sensitive to language, I can avowedly state that language colours one's thinking, willy-nilly. Adrienne Rich gives us food for thought in her essay on modern poetry in Iraq (*Poetry International Web*, July 2003): 'Poetry springs from a nexus of individual and shared experience, above all an experience of location – geophysical realities, visible landscape, spaces marked out by religion, education and politics, poverty, wealth, gender and physiognomy, subordination and independence ...' These are some of the contexts in which we must view the history of literatures and languages in Ireland, and their inter-penetration, and the way we should look at the poetry of other nations in our globalised, multicultural world. Our current Minister for the Arts, John O'Donoghue TD, referring to a Kerry poet says 'Sigerson Clifford was a god' (*The Irish Times*, 15 July 2003). Local and provincial loyalties are still very strong in Ireland. They can be invigorating or smothering, depending on the nature of our mental and emotional antennae. Adjusting these antennae is an art in itself. It is a duty, in fact, if we are to live responsive and responsible lives.

Irish may not have been as crucial to my sense of identity as I once believed it to be. I'm constantly creating and recreating a host of valid identities for myself, including the eponymous entity in a long poem called 'Xolotl' (a name given me by the Chicano poet Francisco X. Alarcón) which appeared in a book called *Syójó* (Cló Iar-Chonnachta, 2001), itself a Japanese folkloric entity, a type of orang-utan inordinately fond of the rice wine, not to mention the eponymous rogue in a recent book of poems, *Eachtraí Krishnamurphy* (Coiscéim, 2003). In many ways, this Krishnamurphy fellow is freer to speak in the society we live in than is the citizen known as Gabriel Rosenstock. Krishnamurphy recenly wrote a Mass, believe it or not. A scandalous thing to those who do not know its author; merely another extension of his spiritual experimentation to those who do. Of course, nobody is going to read it, celebrate it or perform it – so, what's the point? One word: freedom. Where in the world would you find writers who enjoy such freedom? Newspapers don't bother to review us. TG4 refuses to air a book programme. We can say what we like. Nobody's interested. Who will rein us in and say we are too far to the right, too far to the left, too folkloric, too experimental, too spiritual, too materialistic? Nobody. Being invisible, we can come and go like the gentry (by which I mean the fairy folk)! *Aifreann Krishnamurphy* will not have a celebrant or a congregation. A good thing too, maybe. By the way, any student of theosophy will tell you what a mistake it was to abandon the Latin Mass. I'm sure the angels plug their ears when they hear a Mass in English. I know I do, and I'm no angel. Is this some kind of crazed Anglophobia? Not at all. I simply believe that the older languages, Latin, Irish, Greek, Sanskrit, and so on, are more subtle vehicles for prayer and ritual. Working in Irish has made it easier for my own work to resonate with more of a mantric timbre than, I think, would have been possible in English. And what is poetry without music?

I intend to write more in English, as it happens. I will be curious to know, after such a long absence from English, whether my voluminous use of Irish over the past thirty years or so will have any effect on the English I write. Probably not. Will there be the same degree of pleasure involved? No.

Of course, as suggested above, language does colour one's thinking and one's perception of the world. Here's a haiku of mine that got Joint Second Prize in the International Mainichi Haiku Contest 2003:

> *ag sciorradh thar ghoirt na maidine*
> *beireann ga gréine*
> *ar mhún an ghiorria*

> slipping over morning fields
> a sunray
> catches the hare's urine

Such a haiku moment would have been impossible without knowing the Irish phrase, *chomh scaipthe le mún giorria*, meaning 'as scattered as a hare's piss'. The hare urinates on the run, you see.

So, really, that's about the sum of it. Little things like that. The *drúichtín* mentioned above, God bless all slugs! In Zen-Haiku aesthetics one speaks of *hogan-biiki*, sympathy for all that lives, especially the lowliest, the outcast. Irish was a suitable medium in which to cultivate this consciousness. And I'm still bewitched by the words. *Ullastráth* – 'the day before the day before yesterday', *seicimín* – 'the belly-skin that falls down, in well-fed geese, between the legs.' You know, little things like that. Hare's piss. I'm so grateful. Really. I'm grateful that I discovered such things – I'm more than grateful that they discovered me. Maybe I was ready. That's all.

Gaelscoileanna

Pluralism at work in the Irish education system or a continuing problem for successive governments?

Lorcán Mac Gabhann

The growth of Irish-medium schools, or *gaelscoileanna* as they are otherwise known, is undoubtedly one of the major success stories in the struggle to revive the Irish language over the past thirty years. The soaring numbers of new schools being established and the steadily rising number of children attending them has made the headlines on numerous occasions in the print media in recent years.

The vibrant and dynamic movement fuelled by parental involvement and initiative has been hailed by politicians and educationalists alike as a testimony to the educational system's commitment to the Irish language. The fact that the *gaelscoileanna* movement has been exclusively driven by parents, language activists and committed teachers is largely ignored by the establishment. The personal struggles and sacrifices to establish these schools, sometimes in difficult and hostile circumstances, and often in less than desirable surroundings, is never mentioned on the political platforms when the Irish population is told of governmental support for the Irish language as evidenced by the growth of *gaelscoileanna*. If one did not know better, one might almost think that the Department of Education and Science (DES) actually helped and supported parents to develop these schools. Having said all of the above I do not wish to vilify the DES entirely, as it has to be recognised that the long-term financial implications attached to establishing a whole raft of new schools is problematic. However, I wish to explore in this essay where the whole *gaelscoileanna* movement has come from, to share some of my own experiences as the founding member of a *gaelscoil* and as a language activist who has been very active in this whole area for the past ten years, and I wish finally to look at potential problems in the future for this vibrant, dynamic, exciting movement.

For the purposes of clarity, it would be useful to look at a brief history of Irish-medium education in Ireland. Like all educational and linguistic movements it has been moulded and influenced by many events and political decisions outside of its control.

Irish-medium schools have been a central feature of the Irish education system since the foundation of the state. The new Irish state's expressed aim in the 1920s was to restore the Irish language as the daily spoken language of the Irish people. It was decided that this would be achieved through the education system. Successive governments exhorted Irish primary schools to teach as many classes as possible through the medium of Irish, particularly during the first twenty years of the new Irish state. Second-level schools, and their teaching staff, who operated and taught through Irish were given financial rewards and incentives. By 1941, less than twenty years after the foundation of the state, over 55 per cent of all schools, both primary and post-primary, were teaching some if not all classes through the medium of Irish.[1]

Inspired by the ideology of cultural nationalism it was held that the schools ought to be the prime agents in the revival of the Irish language and native traditions, which it held were the hallmarks of nationhood and the basis for independent statehood. Many people held that the schools in the nineteenth century had been a prime cause of the decline of the Irish language; under a native Irish Government the process would have to be reversed.[2]

However, by the early 1960s the aim of restoring the Irish language as the spoken language of the Irish people had been largely abandoned and the educational and political opposition to this policy of compulsory Irish-medium teaching was being acknowledged for the first time.

The aims and policies of extending Irish-medium instruction were restated by the Minister for Education in 1955, but already by that time the complaints of ordinary parents who believed their children's prospects were being blighted by education in a language they could not understand and which offered them no prospects of employment unless they were in the select minority that could afford secondary education were becoming strident and retreat was in progress.[3]

Many schools, both primary and post-primary, abandoned their policy of teaching at least some subjects or classes through the medium of Irish during the 1960s. The numbers of schools teaching solely through Irish plummeted over a decade and a half and by 1973 only eleven primary schools (outside of the Gaeltacht) and five second-level schools were still teaching solely through Irish.

This was undoubtedly a terrible blow to those who were interested in the restoration and protection of the Irish language. By the early 1970s there was now only a small handful of schools producing fluent Irish-speakers outside the Gaeltacht areas. However, as one system was dying another was taking its place, with the emergence of new Irish-medium schools called *gaelscoileanna*, primarily in the Dublin region initially. These schools were established by parents who were by now unhappy with the amount of Irish their children were learning in school. Many of the initial promoters were parents who spoke Irish at home to their children or who had a particular affinity for the language. They needed the support of an educational system that would support and endorse their ideals and so the *gaelscoileanna* movement was born.[4]

The number of schools increased slowly but steadily during the 1970s, with the movement gathering pace during the 1980s and increasing dramatically during the 1990s. The pace of this growth at primary level surpassed all expectations. In thirty years the number of schools climbed from 11 in 1973 to 149 in 2003. The growth at post-primary level has been slightly more laboured, from 5 schools to 33 over the same period. There are now some 30,000 students receiving their education through Irish outside the Gaeltacht.

It seems ironic now that during the period in which the state was willing to fund, promote and support Irish-medium schools, the Irish people's support for these schools waned significantly – particularly by the 1950s and 1960s. The system had to fail and be reborn to ignite a passion for Irish-medium schools among a significant section of Irish society.

The *gaelscoileanna* movement and other Irish-language organisations have often been trenchant in their condemnation of the lack of state support for this educational sector. However, some critical decisions by the Department of Education and Science and some major events did help to shape and foster the *gaelscoileanna* movement in the last twenty years. Unfortunately, there have also been decisions which have sought to damage the movement, which I will outline later in this article.

In the late 1970s, the now defunct Bord na Gaeilge grant-aided a fledgling support organisation for Irish-medium schools – Gaelscoileanna. Although the grand-aid was minimal the results were immediate. The Bord's financial support enabled the organisation to employ a full-time officer. Almost immediately *gaelscoileanna* began to emerge, firstly in urban areas and then elsewhere throughout the country. Through constant lobbying extra concessions were gained for Irish-medium schools at the end of the 1970s, in terms of a more favourable pupil-teacher ratio, extra capitation grants and, most importantly, the decision that the state would in future purchase the sites for new schools and pay 100 per cent of the capital building costs.

Niamh Bhreathnach, the then Minister for Education, published a Green Paper on Education in 1992 which led to the National Forum on Education in Dublin Castle in 1993. For the first time ever, Gaelscoileanna and other organisations such as Educate Together were welcomed as educational partners on the same footing as the churches and the unions. This created an extremely important precedent and has ensured a place for Gaelscoileanna in all talks and policy decisions involving the education partners since then.

Another significant milestone in Gaelscoileanna's development was the establishment of Foras Pátrúnachta na Scoileanna LánGhaeilge (An Foras). Prior to 1993 the only patron available to the founding committees of new *gaelscoileanna* were the Catholic bishops. The founding of An Foras by the organisation Gaelscoileanna, at the request of the promoters of the first multi-denominational *gaelscoil*, gave founding committees a choice not based solely on religion for the first time ever. An Foras is the only educational patronage system in the country today that will accept schools of differing religious ethos, the only condition being that these schools must operate totally through Irish.

The Good Friday Agreement, or the Belfast Agreement as it is more commonly known, was responsible for the establishment of six cross-border bodies, one of which is An Foras Teanga/The Language Agency. The Language Agency has a dual brief carried out by two internal agencies, The Bord of Ulster Scots and Foras na Gaeilge. Foras na Gaeilge (established 1999) very quickly set about funding the organisation Gaelscoileanna, allowing it to expand its range of activities and to provide a more comprehensive service for schools. In fact by trebling the organisation's grant, An Foras Teanga made it possible for the organisation to increase its staff from the original two employees to a team of five full-time officials.

In 2002, An Chomhairle um Oideachas Gaeltachta agus Gaelscolaíochta was established under Article 31 of the Education Act (1998) after a prolonged intensive campaign by Gaelscoileanna, Comhdháil Náisiúnta na Gaeilge and Eagraíocht na Scoileanna Gaeltachta. The role of the Comhairle is to ensure sufficient teaching aids, sufficient research and sufficient support services at both primary and post-primary levels to develop Irish-medium schools in Gaeltacht and non-Gaeltacht areas, as well as teaching of Irish in other schools.[5]

All of the above organisations, in conjunction with Irish-language organisations such as Glór na nGael, Comhdháil Náisiúnta na Gaeilge and Conradh na Gaeilge play a part in the continuing successful development of *gaelscoileanna* in all parts of Ireland.

The establishment of The Commission on School Accommodation (CSA) in 1996 was to have a profound and lasting impact on the growth and future of Gaelscoileanna. The CSA was established in 1996 by Niamh Bhreathnach to advise and report to the Department on future criteria for recognition of proposed schools at primary level, amongst other things.[6]

The CSA might well be compared to a 'sheep in wolf's clothing'. Broadly speaking, the move by the CSA to discuss issues around the establishment of new primary schools was welcomed by the education partners. Gaelscoileanna and Educate Together naively welcomed it as they felt that the needs of their respective sectors could now be addressed. While I cannot personally claim to know how the Catholic Church and the Irish National Teachers' Organisation (INTO) felt about these discussions, it would appear from their submissions to the CSA that they welcomed the opportunity to try to halt the growing numbers of *gaelscoileanna*. The INTO and the Catholic Church have been traditionally opposed to the establishment of *gaelscoileanna* because new schools upset the *status quo* and put their schools in danger. They were clear and unequivocal about their disapproval of the *gaelscoileanna* movement and the establishment of new schools. The Catholic Church queried the need for *gaelscoileanna* at all and maintained that existing schools could provide the same service.

In regard to all-Irish education, CPSMA queried the creation of a distinct network of designated all-Irish schools and suggested that an 'impact study' might be required to establish the impact of new gaelscoileanna on existing schools that could satisfy the linguistic requirement, particularly if existing schools were given the same level of resources as gaelscoileanna.[7]

In the case of the INTO submission it suggested, where parents wished Irish-medium instruction for their children, that they should be given the following range of choices which would not include the provision of a dedicated *gaelscoil*:

- The provision of additional instruction through the medium of Irish in an existing school or schools;
- The establishment of an all-Irish stream within an existing school;
- The establishment of an all-Irish unit within or attached to an existing school;
- The provision of a resource teacher service.[8]

However, both the INTO and the Catholic Primary School Management Association (CPSMA) recommended in their submissions that where parents sought a multi-denominational school that this be investigated fully in order to fulfil the religious needs of the parents. It is my contention that it would not be deemed politically correct to oppose the establishment of a multi-denominational school.

The Steering Group of the CSA, after many months of discussions, eventually recommended stricter enforcement of the regulations then in use for establishing new schools. It made recommendations about numbers, rental allowances for temporary buildings and local contributions for capital funding amongst others. However, one of the most damaging recommendations was that against recognising a rural/urban divide in terms of numbers needed for new *gaelscoileanna*. This effectively meant that founders of new schools in small rural towns had to get the same number of children in order to qualify for recognition as major urban centres did. Quite a number of small schools had opened in previous years, privately funded by parents for the first couple of years until they reached their target numbers. This would no longer be allowed and so it was ensured that the establishment of small rural *gaelscoileanna* was no longer something that could be achieved.

Many of the recommendations of the CSA have since been implemented, some of them beneficial, such as the increased rental allowance for schools who reach certain numbers, but many of them appear to become more draconian every year. The number of criteria that now have to be fulfilled before a school can open is horrendous. The increased costs in looking for architect's plans and health and safety statements will be another obstacle that parents have to face in establishing new schools. If anything the criteria and procedures currently used by the DES are shrouded in a mist of secrecy that continues to change from year to year without warning.

When I, as a parent, decided to set up a *gaelscoil* in a suburb of Dublin in 1995 I thought that the obstacles were huge. I had to find twenty junior infants, a patron, a building, and I had to prove that there would be future support for the school within the local community and a continuing stream of children for years to come. The twelve months that I spent establishing that school has taken years off my life. The criteria on the face of it seemed relatively simple, but the reality of convincing twenty sets of parents that they should entrust the educational future of their four-year-old children to a voluntary committee with little or no experience in the educational sector was enormous. I would like to thank them now publicly and express the hope that their children, now all in post-primary schools, benefited as my own children did. But the most difficult obstacle of all was trying to find a suitable building or site on which to place temporary classrooms. Every empty or partially empty building from Bray to Dundrum to Stillorgan to Sandyford and back up to Kilternan was investigated. The list of organisations approached included the regional headquarters of the ESB, Leopardstown Race Course, various religious orders, the British Ambassador's residence, a local hotel, a local GAA club and lastly De La Salle Palmerston Rugby Club (DLSP). Eventually a site for temporary accommodation was agreed only for the decision to be overturned in late July, five weeks before the *gaelscoil* was to open. The suspicion at the time was that an INTO representative, who feared the effect of another primary school in the area on the numbers of children attending the local national school, encouraged this last minute change of heart. The following weeks were head-wrecking, gut-wrenching and stomach ulcer-inducing as the frantic search for alternative accommodation took place. The burden of responsibility on the shoulders of the voluntary founding committee during this time was truly frightening. After all, parents had placed the educational future of their children in the hands of the committee. Such was the determination of one member that he offered the basement of his home for the first year of the *gaelscoil*. As is often the case, the saviour of the fledgling *gaelscoil* came from the most unlikely of places. De La Salle Palmerston Rugby Club proved itself more community-orientated than most community groups when it offered the clubhouse as a temporary home for the *gaelscoil*.

The untold stories of any person involved in the establishment of a new *gaelscoil* are many and varied. Mine include:

- committing in excess of forty voluntary hours per week during the year prior to the *gaelscoil's* establishment;
- taking time off work to paint the rugby club's hall so that it might in some way resemble a place of education;
- preparing dressing rooms as classrooms on Sunday nights after weekend AIL Division 1 matches during the first year;
- cleaning toilets, on a rota, as there was no money to pay for a cleaner;

- planting trees in the dark, with my brother, on a cold winter night so as to meet with planning regulations on time;
- canvassing thousands of houses on foot in an effort to attract sufficient numbers of children for the *gaelscoil*.

These anecdotes are not unusual and others could tell many more. Although establishing Gaelscoil Thaobh na Coille may have been the most difficult thing I will ever do in my life, it may also be the most rewarding. Of course it was not a lone venture and many others gave their time and expertise freely. It is because of these people that nine permanent teaching-posts have been created in the community and that over two hundred children now converse fluently in Irish on a daily basis throughout the school-year.

My experiences in 1995 were extremely difficult and often hard to endure. The very same difficulties and uncertainties are encountered by founding committees today. Unfortunately, instead of making it easier for people to establish new *gaelscoileanna*, as was envisaged when the CSA was established, the process is becoming even more difficult and more uncertain. In 1995, when the criteria for a new school had been fulfilled, the Department then granted temporary recognition, usually in April or May before the opening of the school the following September. During 2003 this was not the experience of a number of new schools. In all cases the founding committees followed agreed procedure, i.e. finding twenty junior infants who had never been to school, appropriate accommodation and a patron. The Department then granted temporary recognition as each committee fulfilled its obligations. Then suddenly all kinds of unexpected problems arose. Every detail of each founding committee's application for recognition was scrutinised and questions were raised on the most minor of issues. In one case a committee, from its own slim financial resources, sought an architect's report on the safety and suitability of a proposed building for the new school, as requested by the DES. The architect's report stated that the building was sound structurally and safe from hazards and defects. A very positive report one would have thought! But in late July, just a number of weeks before the *gaelscoil* was due to open, the committee received a letter from the Department stating that although the architect's report said that the building was appropriate it did not say that it was appropriate for *educational needs*. As a result of this rather insignificant omission the Department were not going to *activate the recognition* – recognition that the school had already been granted. I consider this type of action by the state hostile to the development of Irish-medium education. At no time had the DES ever mentioned an activation period or had they ever explained that the granting of temporary recognition would be withdrawn or deactivated on such a minor technicality. Even the very mention of activation of already-granted recognition sends shivers down the backs of all those involved in the future development of Irish-medium education. In reality the use of this new term *activate* means that at no time can the founding committee of a new *gaelscoil* be sure that the Department will not pull the plug, even up to the last minute. The Department never explained when it intended to activate granted recognition during 2003. To date they have not said if they intend to use this practice again in future years and if they do, by what date they intend to inform a founding committee of activation of recognition. Without the answers to these questions how are committees supposed to make critical decisions such as:

- when to sign a lease with a landlord;
- when to employ teachers;
- when to order school uniforms and books.

While the DES has the right to grant recognition, or not, it must do so in a manner that is transparent and understood by all concerned.

Earlier in this article I stated that the numbers of Irish-medium post-primary schools have increased at a much slower rate than those at primary level. The reasons for this are complex and it is a question which Gaelscoileanna is currently addressing. One obvious problem is that the requirements of a post-primary school far exceed the requirements of a primary school. The curriculum is more specialised and therefore requires more than one teacher and one classroom at the start. Another problem that exists is that the DES has not published any step-by-step guidelines as to how and in what circumstances a post-primary school may be recognised. This is probably about to change and possibly not to the future benefit of Irish-medium schools. The CSA is currently discussing new criteria for new second-level schools providing education through the medium of Irish. It would appear from presentations given recently at Gaelscoileanna's Annual Conference in November 2003, by representatives of the CSA, that the proposed criteria for new schools in terms of number of pupils required is punitive. As is the experience of the *gaelscoileanna* movement over the years, there seems again to be little support, or sympathy, for the future development of Irish-medium education at this, or any, level from its educational partners on the CSA. If the Government were to accept the current view of the CSA, the future of *gaelscoileanna* at post-primary level would be doomed, except in areas of very high population density, and even in these cases the future would be quite uncertain. How best could the state kill off the future of Irish-medium education, and as a result the best chance there is for the survival of the Irish language, than to ensure that there will be no development at post-primary level? This will be the case if the current thinking of the CSA is adopted by Government. The CSA are considering that no new schools at post-primary level should be recognised by the Department of Education unless they can guarantee thirty pupils in the first year of operation and forty pupils every year after. If this had been state policy over the decades great bastions of Irish-language education such as Coláiste Eoin, Coláiste Íosgáin, Scoil Chaitríona in Dublin,

Coláiste Ailigh in Donegal, Coláiste na Coirbe in Galway and Gaelcholáiste Cheatharlach in Carlow would not now be in existence. In many of these cases the schools were established with pupil numbers as low as ten or twelve. It is well known and accepted that it takes up to five years for the numbers that are now being suggested by the CSA to be achieved in newly-established second-level schools. Again the biggest challenge facing the future of *gaelscoileanna* may come from within Government circles, if these recommendations are introduced by the Minister for Education.

It is difficult to address all the issues surrounding a question as complex as that of the provision of Irish-medium education at all levels from pre-school to university for those who choose it. I have barely scraped the surface in this essay and have mentioned only some of the many complex questions and financial difficulties surrounding this provision. For example, as mentioned earlier, there is undoubtedly a problem with providing buildings for all of these new burgeoning *gaelscoileanna*, but it is my firm belief that instead of saying no to new schools and making life next to impossible for those parents trying to establish new schools, the DES and CSA should be in dialogue with Gaelscoileanna and An Foras about creative ways of providing accommodation. Solutions have to be found to the buildings impasse and it is certainly not good enough to risk the future of our native language by culling and curtailing the growth of the most positive thing to happen to the Irish language in decades.

Notes

1 Gearóid Denvir, *An Ghaeilge, an Ghaeltacht agus 1992*, Glór na nGael, Dublin 1992, p. 9.
2 John Coolahan, *Irish Education: History and Structure*, Institute of Public Administration, Dublin, 1981, p. 38.
3 Reg Hindley, *The Death of the Irish Language*, Routledge, London, 1990, p. 38.
4 Although many of the promoters of the initial schools were Irish-speakers, this is not always true of the *gaelscoileanna* established today.
5 An Chomhairle um Oideachas Gaeltachta agus Gaelscolaíochta, *Plean Stráitéise 2003-2004*, Meitheamh 2003.
6 An Coimisiún um Chóiríocht Scoileanna, *Tuarascáil an Ghrúpa Stiúrtha*, Meán Fómhair 1998.
7 Extract from the submission of the CPSMA to the CSA on the issue of criteria for the recognition of new schools. A Report of the Technical Working-Group, Commission on School Accommodation, Criteria and Procedures for the Recognition of New Primary Schools, January 1988, p. 29.
8 Extract from the INTO submission to the CSA on the issue of criteria and procedures for recognition of new primary schools.

The Irish for Multicultural*

Anna Heusaff

'Nelly Marivate is ainm dom,' says one woman. 'Is as an Afraic mé,' says the man beside her. Both are participants in an Irish-language course organised specifically for asylum-seekers and refugees. A small group of people gathers every Monday morning in Galway to learn a language most of them had hardly heard of just a few years ago.

Some of the class are already multilingual. Josphep's first language is Kikuyu, one of the many languages of his native Kenya, and he also speaks Swahili and English. Lovina speaks her first language, Igbo, to her young son Patrick, as well as English, and growing up in Nigeria she learnt French and German too. Nelly and Merium, both South African, have different native languages.

So for them, learning Irish is less daunting than for people who are used to the sounds of only one language in their heads. Their reasons for spending an hour a week at the class are mixed. Most want to learn more about Irish culture, to understand the country they live in and hope to belong to. They see signposts in Irish and wonder what they mean. Nelly visited Conamara and wanted to be able to speak Irish to people there. And some also want to help their children with homework.

---

* This is a version of an article which first appeared in *The Irish Times*.

The class, which is organised and paid for by Galway's branch of Conradh na Gaeilge, is just one small example of the multiculturalism taking root in Ireland today. People from a great range of cultural backgrounds have brought with them dozens of languages, to add to the major two which we've had for centuries. The future is full of possibilities of diversity and enrichment for all of us – but becoming multicultural isn't just about change in English-speaking Ireland. It's also about attitudes and responses amongst recent immigrants to Irish; and about Irish-speakers' reactions to and links with them.

Multiculturalism is also about a changing image of who the people of this country are. Such change is not new – in fact, it could be said that it's been happening since the first migrant people arrived millenia ago. And recently, viewers of TG4's soap, *Ros na Rún*, have been adding a new face to their image of Irish-speaking Irishness, with the arrival of a character played by actor Séamas Ó Feithcheallaigh. Séamas grew up in an institution in Clifden, but spent periods as a teenager in a Gaeltacht summer college and with an Irish-speaking foster family in Clondalkin. Ever since then, he's been used to people's surprise at hearing a black person speak Irish fluently.

'I'm a *Gaeilgeoir*,' he says, 'it's part of my life, no more than for anyone else who grew up with the language. But I meet Irish speakers who assume that because of the colour of my skin, they have to speak English to me. Of course, they stop being surprised once they get to know me. So I expect to get some similar reactions to my character in *Ros na Rún*. I'm glad to say, though, that I'm not typecast in the series, as an immigrant doctor, for example. I'm just another Irish person, as I am in real life.'

Séamas Ó Feithcheallaigh is of the same generation as Paul McGrath and Kevin Sharkey, black Irish people who've been part of this country's life for decades now. The fact that there are more and more Irish people whose backgrounds include African, Asian, East European and other origins is a natural progression, in his view. And it's just as natural that some of them will speak Irish.

Ó Feithcheallaigh doesn't fit the stereotype of a *Gaeilgeoir*. That may be a challenge to those who like to think in little boxes; and similarly, according to Piaras Mac Éinrí, Ireland's expanding multiculturalism is a challenge to a deep-rooted intolerance here. Mac Éinrí, who founded the Migration Studies Centre in Cork, says that many Irish people are intolerant not only of colours and cultures from faraway places, but of homegrown diversity as well. The two can be linked, in his view. 'Every day,' he says, 'I come across people who can't even be bothered to spell my name properly. So how are they going to show respect to more unfamiliar names from other cultures? And therefore to the people who carry those names?'

Other Irish speakers echo Mac Éinrí's link between their own experiences of being treated as an exotic sub-species, or as a nuisance, and those of recent immigrants who are marginalised because they're seen as 'different'. Another common link could be the effort involved for families trying to bring up children bilingually in a sea of English. Then there's the provision of official information and services in languages other than English, not to mention cultural and language sensitivity – whether in *Gaeltachtaí* or amidst the Chinese, Romanian or other communities – in the health and education systems.

There are difficult questions to be asked, however, about links between Irish and multiculturalism. For example, should *gaelscoileanna* – many of which are oversubcribed already – reach out to new communities to enrol children whose background is not ethnic Irish? If they don't, will their pupils grow up in bastions of 'cultural whiteness', unrepresentative of the society around them? On the other hand, when it comes to questions of status and resources, how could Irish, which is woven into the history and fabric of this country's life, be on a par with recently-arrived languages?

And now that 6 per cent of the population are nationals of other countries, what about the requirement for Irish for certain jobs? Many immigrants – who express goodwill towards Irish in general – ask, for example, whether all Gardaí should be competent in Irish, or all teachers of children with special needs. This is not to sideline the needs of Irish-speakers, but to ask for flexibility in the recruitment of people educated outside of Ireland, so that they are not automatically excluded.

So there's plenty of debate on the horizon, which many Irish-language organisations – and others – are barely waking up to. Being multicultural is not an easy ride for any society, but it's also a reality – to a greater or lesser extent – for most. Meanwhile, Piaras Mac Éinrí argues that all immigrants should be offered short familiarisation courses, to give them an overview of Ireland's history, languages, cultures and workings. People can hardly be expected to 'integrate', he says, without offering them a door to understanding what makes the country tick.

It was just such a familiarisation tour of Galway, organised by the city's Refugee Support Group, which initiated contact between them and Conradh na Gaeilge. Participants were fascinated to find out about Irish, and following a number of shared workshops in African and traditional Irish music and dance, Nelly Marivate carried out voluntary research to establish the level of interest amongst asylum-seekers and refugees in learning Irish. Not everyone was positive, of course, and some asked why they should learn Irish when so many people native to Ireland don't speak it.

It's nothing new, of course, for foreigners from many backgrounds to learn Irish, through Conradh and other groups. What's striking is the range of forms taken by such contacts now. A beginners' class focused on recent immigrants also started recently in Dublin, and there may be other such initiatives around the country. Then there's the sideways take on an outsider's experience of the language, provided by the short film which won awards and encomiums during 2003. *Yu Ming is Ainm Dom* tells of a Chinese student who is determined to travel to Ireland, and who proudly masters the country's first official language before his departure. Comedy and confusion ensue when he tries to speak it on the streets upon his arrival there. A clever and engaging story in itself, which also throws our society's ambivalence about Irish into sharp relief.

The contacts made in Galway also provide a reminder of the global context of struggles for language survival. 'My own language, Kikuyu, is spoken less and less by young people in urban areas,' according to Josphep. The same threat of extinction hangs over hundreds, even thousands, of other languages around the world. Indeed, contrary to that outdated stereotype of the *Gaeilgeoir* who sees the language as a bulwark against the outside world, many Irish-speakers say they're motivated by a commitment to diversity and cultural freedoms everywhere.

Finally, a small personal example of change. I grew up in an Irish-speaking family in Dublin a few decades ago. Chatting on a bus with my siblings often entailed bearing up to stares, whispers or exclamations from people nearby. Even when strangers heaped praise upon us – as they frequently did – we could feel we were viewed as exhibits.

My perception is that these attitudes have changed subtly in recent years. When I speak Irish to my young son on today's Dublin bus, I no longer feel I'm stared at – because these days, we're surrounded by people speaking Latvian, Russian, French, and Portuguese. Being different, in whatever way, is a more comfortable experience when lots of other people are different too.

Passing the Torch to the Next Generation

Pádraig Ó Mianáin

It's not easy, being an Irish speaker. It's not easy anywhere in the country, even in the Gaeltacht areas, but here in the North, I can tell you, it can be bloody hard. There is nothing as strange as feeling like an absolute stranger in your own land because you speak your own language.

When asked if I would offer a contribution to this book to give a northerner's view of the world *as Gaeilge*, I was reluctant at first. These kind of books tend to be the preserve of literary and cultural types and mine would be a fairly ordinary piece, as I consider myself a fairly ordinary man with fairly ordinary interests. It would be a lot easier for me to write this in Irish, being a *cainteoir dúchais* (native speaker of Irish) to whom all expression in English is a process of translation. Also, the language can be like religion in that one can be very committed to it in a personal or private way without shouting it from the rooftops; it would be very easy to slip unintentionally into proselytising mode, a pet hate of mine, or else come across as a lost romantic.

Upon reflection, however, I felt that all those reasons for not doing it were, conversely, valid reasons for doing it. Let it be seen that Irish-speakers in the North see themselves as 'ordinary'; if others see us as extraordinary on account of our language, then so be it. And if English doesn't flow from my pen as fluently as Irish does, then let it be known that there exist people like me whose first language is Irish. And as to baring one's cultural soul, it's no harm if it gives an insight into the mind of a modern Irish-speaker; for the Irish-speaking community is often accused of being very introverted, of opening few windows for the outside world to look in and see what it's all about. As for approval or disapproval of my view of things, the first thing any Irish-speaker needs to survive is a healthy layer of very thick skin.

I'm not your typical Irish-speaking northerner. All I can represent is my own experience of the language here. The typical Irish-speaking northerner is either someone who made a conscious decision to become an Irish-speaker or, a minority within the minority, someone who was raised in an Irish-speaking family here or is a product of the Irish-medium education system. I, on the other hand, was raised in the Donegal Gaeltacht and was fifteen by the time my family moved to Derry, by which point my linguistic formation as a native speaker was complete. I can't tell you what Irish added to or changed in my life, for it was always there; I can't say what inspired or drove me to learn the language, as I knew the language before I knew I knew it, if you get my drift. I can't speak for the experience of children raised through Irish here, as their experiences are totally different from mine, and perhaps more interesting or pertinent than mine. Whatever the difficulties of the language in the traditional *Gaeltachtaí*, it is a doddle compared to here. Essentially, though, their diverse experiences and mine highlight the same fundemental fact, that of our existence.

Being brought up in the South gave me a different view of the circumstances affecting the language here. Anyone who is born in the North adapts subconsciously to the political and sectarian realities of life; it is often said that people here have become immune or desensitised to what goes on around them. The same must apply to the Irish-speakers in the North – when they meet with hostility or discrimination of a political or sectarian nature, the fact that they are used to it acts as a buffer against its full effect. Coming from the South, though, I had no concept of this dimension of the language issue, and its impact on me was quite profound. Sure, in the South, you'll come across apathy and resentment towards the language, and at times some hostility, but rarely, if ever, would speaking the language or being identified as an Irish-speaker place you in any physical danger.

Here in the North, there are many reasons why people learn and speak Irish. To some, it is a form of resistance against British occupation and against the Anglicising ethos that is so pervasive in every facet of life. Not only is Irish, then, a sign of casting off the cultural shackles of colonisation, but it is also a direct V-sign to the establishment that despite the odds, the natives have not all been 'civilised'. In effect, every person who speaks Irish bears witness to the failure of centuries of cultural cleansing by the establishment in Ireland.

Others, who might not be so militantly exercised by party politics but who would be of a strongly nationalist mind, feel that the language is a part of the identity they were denied a proper opportunity to explore when they were younger, whether in the education system or in their social environment. Irish was very much *lingua non grata* during the Troubles, and lots of people, particularly in areas that weren't considered safe, were reluctant to be openly associated with the language as it marked you out as a Catholic. Even now, speaking Irish or having an Irish name is fraught with danger in the wrong areas; however dangerous it might be to have a distinctive accent in English, Irish leaves no doubt whatsoever about who you are and which side you belong to.

There are others whose interest in Irish is fuelled purely by the satisfaction or pleasure they derive from their enhanced appreciation and understanding of their surroundings, whether they be interested in local history, in placenames, in traditional lore and pastimes, in songs or stories, or for those who master the language, the beauty and style of the language itself. Regardless of their own political affiliations or lack thereof, the language doesn't affect their views on The Problem. Most of the Protestants/Unionists who learn the language would fall into this category; they realise that it doesn't make you any more or less Protestant/Unionist, and indeed this was the view of leaders of the vibrant Presbyterian movement for the Irish language in Belfast and beyond in the late eighteenth and nineteenth centuries.

In recent times, a new grouping has emerged within the Irish-speaking community: people who were raised in Irish-speaking families or who have come through the Irish-medium education system and who see Irish as either their first language or as being of equal status with English as their language. Whatever about what motivated their parents, this new breed would have been too young to ponder the philosophy of the language question; as the ad says, they just do it. How profound an effect this new phenomenon will have on the future of the language here won't be known until we see how many second and third generation speakers come from this first generation, but regardless of what may transpire in the future, they are here right now and deserve to be included in their own right.

The language issue is essentially a question of identity; here, everything is a question of identity. To the Irish-speaking community, the language is at the core of their identity; to a lot of others in the wider community, Irish doesn't matter either way. To the majority, though, the Irish language is the antithesis of what they feel everybody's identity should be. At best, Unionists will tolerate the language as long as it doesn't in any way involve them, and at worst, the reaction to the Irish language is that of a fussy gardener who finds weeds cropping up again despite his best efforts at rooting them out. Around the time of the first ceasefire, a prominent Unionist politician came to give a lecture in the College where I work, a brave thing to do, and in itself an early indication of the new dispensation. During the post-lecture discussion, he was asked whether he saw himself as British or Irish. He sort of shuffled around the question, and gave the impression that he saw himself as both and neither at the one time. The Unionist community appear at times to find it much easier to define what they definitely are not than what they actually are.

In the North, being an Irish-speaker has long been seen as a badge of militant republicanism. This has led to the language being demonised as 'the language of the bomb and the bullet', as it was described on one television programme I was in the audience for. I have no idea what percentage of those wielding guns during the Troubles were Irish-speakers, but you can be fairly sure that every single one of them, republican, loyalist, police and British army alike, was an English-speaker. Would English then, one might ask, not be more deserving of the 'bomb and bullet' mantle?

For those hostile to the language, the link between the republican movement and the language has long been a stick with which to beat the language. Within the nationalist community, it became a perfect opt-out excuse for many who might otherwise be seen to be neglecting their duty towards the language. Republicans are just as entitled as anybody else to be involved in the language, and the language is certainly much less lethal than other weapons in their armoury. Sure, I resent the way they seek to use the language and the language community to further their own political agenda, just as I would resent any grouping doing likewise, but for me, the problem is not that republicans monopolise the language – a fallacy in itself – but that other major players such as the Catholic Church, the GAA and the SDLP, have – with respect to individuals within those organisations who do what they can – been marked largely absent when leadership and political direction was needed on language issues. For a lot of people, it was easier to sit on the high moral fence than to get involved on the ground.

What, then, is it like to live your life as an Irish-speaker in the North? I'm very fortunate in that Irish is the language of home and work, the two main components in daily life. The fact that my wife, Susan, is also an Irish-speaker is a huge advantage, particularly as we are raising our daughter, Cliodhna, through

Irish. It remains to be seen how the linguistic divide will play on Cliodhna's future, as she is still at the 'goo-goo' language stage, but the chances of her making it through to her teens with Irish as her first language are greatly increased because Irish is the sole language in the house. The fact that Irish is the spoken language at my workplace is also a big plus. The mixture of people working there, their varied interests and backgrounds, and in particular the fact that we are all fully fluent in Irish, means that the language is used (and often abused) just like any other language would be. The benefits of Irish being spoken at home and at work cannot be overstated – without at least one of these, it is impossible to 'live' the language.

That, however, is where the positives end. Outside of home and work – and I emphasise again that I'm exceptionally fortunate in both these regards – all other aspects of ordinary life are not available in Irish. We live in Portstewart on the Derry/Antrim border, an area not particularly renowned for the celebration of cultural diversity or for the promotion of all that is historically native to the area; it'll be some time, I fear, before we see any bilingual streetsigns around here. There are only a half dozen people in the area who speak Irish, all 'blow-ins' and the majority of whom came to the area via the nearby university in Coleraine; although the number of pupils choosing Irish as a subject in the local secondary schools is increasing, precious few so far have taken it beyond their exams. As far as I know, we are the only Irish-speaking family – where Irish is the only language spoken among both parents and children – within a thirty or forty mile radius, which won't help the process of normalising the language in Cliodhna's eyes when she gets older. The nearest Sunday Mass in Irish is in Derry, and if I need to sort out any other business with the Lord above, the nearest priest who could assist me is about the same distance away. Apart from the principle involved, I don't know any prayers in English, and even if I did, to pray to God in a strange language would be like praying to a strange god. There are no crèches in Irish in the North, as far as I know, and the nearest Irish-medium pre-schools or primary schools are about forty minutes away. There is absolutely no other facility or service, essential or otherwise, available to us through Irish in this area. Basically, apart from home and work, and whenever I happen to meet one of the other Irish-speakers, every aspect of life is through English.

Being an Irish-speaker, then, gives you an insight into the mind of ethnic minorities and the difficulties they meet in the most basic activities in life. I'm constantly asked what my name is in English, as though my name is some form of eccentric idiosyncracy like your man, the popstar, who changed his name to a symbol. Ironically, Catholics/nationalists are the worst at this, as they presume to try and translate it anyway, without as much as a 'by your leave'. Having a name and surname in Irish is like having a strange foreign name, except that foreigners would be more likely to be politely asked to confirm the spelling of their name, and are highly unlikely to be asked what it is in English. It's bad enough having an 'Ó' surname and explaining the intricacies of Mianáin with the accent on the second 'a' (we're talking a seriously monoglot mind here), but try explaining that my wife's surname is Uí Mhianáin, and my daughter is Ní Mhianáin, and you soon realise just how foreign a language Irish is to the vast majority of people. Except, of course, that this is Ireland and that the surname is Irish.

In the South, whether or not people agree with the position of Irish as a subject in the education system, at least most people are familiar to some extent with the language; it is found on roadsigns, state bodies often have Irish names and it is quite common to have an Irish name or surname. In the North, however, the Irish language is non-existent within the primary and secondary state (Protestant) school system and within the Catholic primary school system, and only a minority of pupils in Catholic secondary schools study it to any exam level. To most people in either community in the North, then, even the most basic of phrases in Irish would be as foreign as Greek or Spanish.

The profile of the language has benefited from the post-Agreement thawing of attitudes, but there is a long way to go before Irish will be recognised by all as a cultural resource rather than a political label.

This unfamiliarity with the language may be frustrating, but it is insignificant compared to the naked sectarian aggression you can encounter. Apart from the occasional cultural exchange with the old RUC – I haven't yet had occasion to test the new culture in policing here – where I was a cert to be hassled every time because I dared to give them my proper name (they seemed to object to my assertion that the English version of my name is 'Mr Pádraig Ó Mianáin'), I've been attacked or threatened on a couple of occasions in my local area for no reason other than for speaking Irish. Once, whilst engaged in a conversation with a colleague as we walked along the local promenade, one of the local intelligentsia kindly reminded us, *en passant*, that we were in 'Ulster' now and he urged his companions to throw these Fenians into the harbour; on another occasion, another local champion of civil liberties took great offence at myself and another friend speaking in Irish on the local bus and proceeded to try to empty the contents of an ashtray over us while ranting on about Fenians and so on. These were totally unprovoked attacks, as on both occasions we were minding our own business and were not even aware that somebody was taking any notice of us. Whilst the tragic lack of functional grey matter evident in both cases must be taken into account, there are plenty of fools like these and they can be very dangerous, particularly when your family also become 'legitimate targets'.

In the grand scheme of things, and certainly in the context of what many others have suffered during the Troubles, these incidents are fairly minor. Neither incident was reported to the police, as at times it's better to let idiots like that have their rant than to further draw their attention to you by reacting. And I acknowledge fully that sectarian abuse happens in both directions. That shouldn't, however, take away from the impact of incidents such as these that are a reality of daily life for Irish-speakers. We are still some way away from a situation here where one could speak Irish in public without attracting unwelcome attention. Whether you like it or not, you take a stance when you speak Irish here in the North, a place full of wrong places and wrong times.

Why on earth, you may ask, would we wish to raise our child through Irish in such a difficult environment? As a gesture of defiance against the *status quo*? As a sacrificial lamb on the altar of the language? Just to be different? Out of sheer lunacy? This is a question we asked ourselves as well, because it's not a decision any parent can take lightly. And no, it isn't about defiance or sacrificial lambs or a desire to be different. As for the lunacy bit, who can tell? After all, there is little difference between *Gaeltacht* and *gealtacht* (lunacy). Ultimately, the question is not 'Why Irish?' but 'Why not Irish?' There is no just reason for denying our child her right to be brought up in her own language. If we, her parents, regard the language as being central to our identity, to how we define ourselves and our attachment to the country in which we live, to its history and to its culture and traditions, then why shouldn't we raise our child accordingly? To do otherwise would be unnatural.

This is not the place, nor am I the man, to convince people of the merits and virtues of the Irish language; to some extent, if they can't see it for themselves, it's like trying to explain the value of music to a deaf man. Suffice it to say, in the context of a northerner, that the benefits of the language are just as pertinent here as anywhere else in Ireland; indeed, we have an added benefit here given the dialectal link with Scottish Gaelic. Many placenames here are of Irish origin, and Irish was still spoken in many areas in the North only a hundred years ago. When you factor in the proud tradition of Protestant involvement in the language from the sixteenth century up to, again, a hundred years ago, you find that you don't have to dig too deep to unearth a rich vein of heritage common to both traditions. The Irish language predates the religious divide, and there is no reason why it shouldn't outlive it.

The question of the language as an essential component in the national identity is quite a contentious one; it all depends on how you define 'Irish' identity. Personally, I can't see how one can truly understand our history and tradition without a sound knowledge of Irish. It's like saying that Irish history and literature began around the early nineteenth century, when the native language was torn from its roots in the psyche of the people and replaced within one or two generations by a language foreign to them. Without Irish, all you have is a *scéal scéil* (a second-hand account) instead of the real *scéal* – at best, a black and white sketch of the full colour masterpiece. As the Basque proverb says, 'If you don't know where you're coming from, you don't know where you're going', and that is the fundamental reason for raising our child through Irish: to enable her to see the story in full colour and work out her own cameo role within it.

Cultural identity is a state of mind, and there is no reason to feel like second-class citizens of the modern world just because we are a numerical minority. A teacher who taught in the primary school on Rathlin Island, a few miles from here, once told me of a young boy who wrote in an essay that 'Ireland is a large island off the coast of Rathlin'. The relative size of the island didn't matter to him; that was just how he saw the universe from his point of view. That's the attitude with which we, the Irish-speaking community, should view the world, confident in our own identity and able to meet other cultures as equals. It's about who we are, not who we want to be or don't want to be. My wife and I feel that bringing our daughter up secure in her own identity while teaching her to respect other identities is the best preparation we can provide her with as she grows up to find her own bearings in life. We can always hope that better times lie ahead and that the path of the Irish-speaker through life will get smoother. Whatever happens, all we can do is pass the torch on to the next generation and wish them Godspeed.

Idir Dhá Theanga:
Irish-language Culture and the
Challenges of Hybridity

Máirín Nic Eoin

In this article I wish to address two inter-related questions which I believe are now among the most important cultural questions facing Irish-speakers (and any Irish person with an interest in the language and its fate). These are the question of cultural hybridity and the question of linguistic change. In relation to the first, the crucial issue is whether Irish-language culture can be defined and located, or should we accept that, like all living phenomena, Irish-language culture is being constantly redefined and relocated, as it attempts to maintain a recognisable presence in an increasingly hybridised national culture. The question of linguistic change relates to the contact-induced change within the language itself occurring both in Gaeltacht and non-Gaeltacht contexts. The Irish language is changing, but is this change to be welcomed as a sign of vitality or is it a sign of impending obsolescence and death? In attempting to tease out these issues I will draw on the work of a number of contemporary Irish-language writers.

Donegal poet Cathal Ó Searcaigh published a poem on the cusp of the millennium called *'Trasnú'* (Traversing) which is a humorous celebration of the hybrid state in which the Irish language finds itself, 'ar strae/ áit inteacht/ idir Cath Chionn tSáile/ agus an *Chinese takeaway*,' (astray somewhere between the Battle of Kinsale and the *Chinese takeaway*). The strands of our story are all mixed up', and what the poem does is to outline what some of these strands are in the form of an interlingual litany of interculturality. The poem ends on the following note:

Tá muid teach ceanntuíach
agus bungaló mod conach;
Tá muid seanbhean bhochtach
Agus Marilyn Monroeach;
Tá muid scadán gortach
agus takeaway microwave*ach;*
Tá muid seanscéal báiníneach
agus scoopscéal Sky*-ach;*
Tá muid turas an tobaireach
agus rock 'n roll walkman*ach;*
Tá muid dún daingeanach
agus mobile home*ach;*
Tá muid carr capallach
agus Vauxhall Cavalier*-each;*
Tá muid béadán baileach
agus porn internet*ach;*
Tá muid bairín breacach
agus pina colada cheesecake*ach;*
Tá muid rince seiteach
agus hócaí pócaí cairiócaíach.

Tá muid ag fí ár dtodhchaí as ár ndúchas;
ag Magee-áil ár mbréidín brocach buí,
ag Levi-áil ár mbrístí de chorda an rí,
Ó, tá muid ag fí ár dtodhchaí as ár ndúchas.'

In this poem the mixture is celebrated. The fact that we can accommodate global cultural products while still retaining contact with the local and the native is seen as a sign of vitality, of creative energy, of the ability to adapt (rather than succumb) to cultural pressure: 'We are weaving our future from our past.' The image of hybridity to emerge from the poem could and should be critiqued on a number of grounds, however. The issue of cultural power (and its links to economic power) would need to be examined, for example. Who gets to decide what goes into the intercultural mix? Also the depiction of native, local, Gaelic culture in the poem could be seen to link that culture to the past, to what would now be looked upon as traditional, old-fashioned and folkloristic, while the contemporary and cosmopolitan is represented in terms of what has been foisted on us, *dár ndeoin nó dár n-ainneoin*, due to processes of globalisation. This is a view of Irish-language culture which would be rejected by many Irish-speakers who resent the association of the language with images from the past, preferring to see it as a modern adaptable medium capable of representing any number of social situations and lifestyles.

The clever juxtapositions in the poem, however, do succeed in foregrounding the hybrid nature of contemporary Irish-speaking Ireland. The question many people might ask is where will the Irish language end up in the face of ever more vigorous processes of hybridisation. For Ó Searcaigh, this question is irrelevant as he is not interested in final destinations as much as in the journey itself. Fundamental to his notion of culture is the sense that identity is not something stable and unchanging. Rather it is mobile, constantly changing, in a process of renegotiation. It is more concerned with crossing boundaries – *trasnú* – than with defending them, with opening up to other cultures than with closing down the shutters. Such a view is in tune with the positive reading of hybridity in the work of many contemporary cultural critics – most notably post-colonial critic Homi Bhabha, who has defined the colonial and post-colonial subject very much in terms of hybridity (that both the coloniser and the colonised are inextricably implicated in one another's sense of identity); cultural critic Stuart Hall who accepts as positive the inevitably hybrid identities of the Afro-Caribbean diaspora; and feminist philosopher Rosi Braidotti who, in her discussion of female subjectivity in her aptly-named book

Nomadic Subjects, links the concept of hybridity to the notion of identity as fluid, unstable, non-fixed, nomadic.

As an Irish-language writer, Ó Searcaigh is not alone in his awareness of multiculturality and the challenges of border-crossing. A recurring concern in the work of contemporary Gaeltacht writers Micheál Ó Conghaile and Pádraig Ó Cíobháin is also this question of accommodating change, of movement in and out of traditional communities, of negotiating relationships between the urban and the rural. In comparing 1990s' Conamara to the Conamara of the 1960s, Ó Conghaile is optimistic about the ability of the community to grapple with the challenges of the intercultural mix:

> *Is Conamara de chineál eile ar fad atá againn anois. Conamara an* disco, *an* rock an' roll, *an* chountry and western, *an* walkman *agus an* chairiócaí. *Conamara na* night clubs, *na* bpotholes *agus na* mobile homes. *Conamara na* videos, *Conamara* Chablelink, *Conamara Sky agus na* satailítí. *Conamara 'Home and Away' agus 'Choronation Street', Conamara an* bhingo, *na* lotteries. *Conamara an chócó cola, na* hotels, *na* chippers. *Conamara an microwave, na* mud wrestlers *agus an* Sunday World.
>
> *Seo é ár gConamara, an Conamara atá á shú isteach agus á análú againn chuile lá. An Conamara atá fórsaí móra an tsaoil ag brú orainn uaireanta, agus uaireanta eile an Conamara a bhfuil go leor againn féin ag glacadh leis go fonnmhar, an Conamara nua atá muid a chruthú dúinn féin. Seo é ár gcultúr anois, nach cultúr amháin é ach cultúir. Uaireanta is ar éigean a aithníonn muid muid féin sa tranglam.*[2]

This acceptance and celebration of interculturality is a new element in Irish-language writing and there are very good reasons why the subject was not discussed to any considerable degree until recently. For long the Irish language was looked upon and presented not just as 'part of what we are' but as the very bedrock of national identity, as encapsulated in phrases such as *'Tír gan teanga, tír gan anam'*. Cultural nationalism was always concerned with establishing what made a culture different and distinctive (even if that often involved a certain amount of invention of tradition). Language was seen as the most fundamental of cultural markers. Without the Irish language, or so the argument went, we would be less distinctive, less essentially ourselves. But if the Irish language can no longer be seen as a bearer of a distinctive pure culture, if it is merely to be seen as one element (and perhaps not the dominant one) in an intercultural mix, well then do we really lose anything if we lose it? It is a difficult question to answer. My own view is that we would lose that creative dynamic which comes into play when the perspectives of more than one language are brought to bear on any particular cultural situation. In the context of the globalisation of English, we would lose that ability to negotiate on our own terms between the local and the global; instead of being able to accommodate the global and adapt the local, we would be in danger of becoming truly provincial, mimicking the most dominant forms of anglophone culture. With such a prospect Conamara country-and-western would be an imitation of American country-and-western; the Máimín Cajun band would be unthinkable; and Gearóid Mac Lochlainn would not get to harness the energies of contemporary rap to the sounds and rhythms of Belfast Irish. Losing Irish would not merely involve the severing of a link with our cultural past, but would also limit the possibilities for new kinds of cultural fusion in the future.

The language revival, of course, was a central component in an anti-colonial enterprise, and was seen as an attempt at retrieving that which had been lost, and, most importantly, to revalorise that which had been devalorised historically. The project was a radically ambitious one, and enthusiasm for it was not shared by all. There were alternative views even within cultural nationalism. The dominant view to emerge in Anglo-

Irish literary circles was the idea that language revival was not necessary for the Irish people to retain a distinct identity because Irish English was distinctive enough to ensure that national identity was not lost through language shift. To echo Nigerian writer Chinua Achebe, English, it was felt, 'could bear the weight of our Irish cultural experience.' Such a view has been expressed by many writers and critics, and is the theme of a 1983 Field Day pamphlet by Tom Paulin, *A New Look at the Language Question*. The view that the language of the coloniser can be appropriated and creatively used for their own ends by the colonised is now almost an orthodoxy within post-colonial criticism, and attempts to argue in favour of the use of, or return to, indigenous languages as literary media are often attacked as smacking of essentialism and narrow-minded nationalism. The question of language rights and language choice are seldom given due recognition and neither is the relationship between writers and the communities they seek to reach or to represent. For many Irish-language writers, it is by accentuating their difference, and by demanding cultural space for that which they have been at pains to retrieve, that they hope to survive in a climate where Hiberno-English is seen to be the hardier hybrid.

It is not surprising, therefore, that Ó Searcaigh's easy celebration of hybridity has not been possible for many Irish-language writers. I think that an individual's attitude to cultural hybridity can usually be explained in terms of that individual's sense of cultural confidence. For Ó Searcaigh, a Gaeltacht writer and native speaker of Irish firmly anchored in a particular community, instability and mobility are not threats to his own sense of cultural and linguistic belonging. It is his sense of belonging which allows him to explore, to traverse boundaries, to embark on creative voyages of exploration. Such freedom is not enjoyed by Irish-language writers whose cultural experience has been one of deracination, or whose sense of themselves is linked inextricably to a sense of deep cultural loss. Armagh poet, Aodh Ó Murchú, of an older generation than Ó Searcaigh, responded in highly emotive terms to Ó Searcaigh's *'Trasnú'*, which he described in his own poem *'Dúchas na Cinniúna'* (Fateful Heritage) as an outburst and as an act of betrayal. Ó Murchú, living in an English-speaking region and cut off by a generation from contact with the last local native speakers of Irish, imagines the role of a Gaeltacht writer such as Ó Searcaigh as one of vigilance. He should never cross over to the other side, but should remain on this side as a witness.

Nuair a fheanntar dúchas an duine
Siar go dtí cnámh is carraig,
Gan fágtha roimhe ach taise
Ar foluain sna cnoic is sna creaga,
gan fágtha dá theanga ach gluaiseanna
Fuaimscríofa ar imeall logainmneacha,
Gach coiscéim a thugann sé uaidh
Caithfear gur chun tosaigh a chosa.
Rugadh mise as an chinniúint
A fheiceann tusa romhat ar an bhealach,
Dorn do bhuile tógtha
In éadan tonnta na staire.

Tá tú seasta anois ar an chladach,
Ag bagairt ar thuilte na mara,
tréigint do dhúchais is do chine
ina riastradh sa dán nua TRASNÚ.
Réitigh do sceadamán den déistin
Is treoraigh as an nua do theanga.
Ní dual duit mar fhile go deo trasnú,
Ach fanacht i bhfos id'fhinné.

Thugas-sa na céimeanna beaga
gach céim acu ina chúis lúcháire
Mar níor fágadh agamsa ach sléibhte,
As a bhfaighinn mo rithim, is creaga,

'Who Needs Irish?'

Cainteoir deireannach mo dhúchais
i dtost na mblianta tharam.
Ar bhlár na deise a cailleadh,
Mé seasta liom féin go balbh,
Gan fágtha agam ach riascra
As a ngreannfainn mo fhriotal is teanga.

[When a person's heritage is cut
Back to bone and rock,
With nothing left but a ghost
Lingering in hill and crag.
When one's tongue lives only in soundglosses
written on the edge of placenames,
every step one takes
has to be a step forward.
I was born of the fate
You see before you on the way,
Your fist held up
Against the waves of history.

You are standing now on the shoreline,
Threatening the ocean's floods,
the desertion of your tradition and your tribe
like an outburst in your new poem TRAVERSING.
Clear your throat of its nausea
And guide again your tongue.
As a poet you should never cross over
But remain on this side as a witness.

I took the small steps
each step a cause for joy
As I was only left with mountains,
as sources of my rhythm, and crags,
the last speaker of my native place
silent for years before me.

On the plain of lost chances,
I stood alone and mute,
Left only with moorland
From which I'd shape my speech and tongue.]

Many Irish-language writers of non-Gaeltacht background have been troubled by the question of their own cultural position. Feeling cut off historically and geographically from Gaeltacht culture, some of them became obsessed with a sense of being forever outsiders, on the margins both of mainstream English-speaking Ireland and of the Gaelic culture to which they were so attracted and devoted. The question *'Cá bhfuil Éire?'* was one which intrigued Seán Ó Ríordáin, though his sense of being linguistically outside of Gaelic culture was ultimately resolved when he embraced the notion of a private language, an individual mode of expression, developed from – but avoiding the constrictions of – the local regional dialect which would form its base. The sense of being a spokesman for a community under threat is pervasive in Ó Ríordáin's journalistic work, and no writer in Irish has escaped the tensions associated with the language's endangered position. Some have described the position of the marginalised and minoritised Irish-speaker as that of being a stranger in one's own land, an alien washed up, ironically, on one's own shore. A very fine poem called *'Trén bhFearann Breac'* (Through the Speckled Land) by Cork poet Colm Breathnach describes the unenviable position of an Irish-speaker travelling through a landscape which serves to constantly remind him of the inferior position of his language and of his own helplessness to do anything about it. The poem opens as follows:

Ní labhraíonn sí a thuilleadh liom, an áit seo,
is níl aon bhuanaíocht ag mo theanga níos mó inti.

Níor chuaigh mo phréamhacha síos ach fad áirithe
is táid ag dreo anois cheal taca uaithi.

Caitheadh salann ar an scraith uachtair
is treabhadh síos é go dtí an t-íochtar.

Ní féidir léi tál a thuilleadh ar a muirín
ar mo thalamh féin is fás coimhthíoch mé.

[She no longer speaks to me, this place,
And my language no longer finds sustenance in her.

My roots only went down so far
and now they are rotting due to lack of support from her.

Salt was thrown on the surface layer
and it was deep ploughed to base.

She can no longer feed her family
on my own land I am a strange growth.]

The recognition given to Irish on the way serves to underline
rather than abate the sense of cultural inferiority:

Ar an mbóthar idir dhá chathair
go bhfuil dhá ainm ar gach ceann acu
léim na focail ar na comharthaí.

Táim ag taisteal trén bhfearann breac
is tá dhá ainm ar gach aon bhaile ann.

Claonadh – Clane
Cill Dara – Kildare
Baile Dháith – Littleton
Cúil an tSúdaire – Portarlington

an t-ainm dúchais
sa chló iodálach

claoninsint ar stair na háite,
an t-ainm dúchais
sa chló is lú
faoninsint ag dul ó chlos…

[On the road between two cities
which each bear two names
I read the words on the roadsigns.

I am travelling through the speckled land
and every town there has two names.

Claonadh – Clane
Cill Dara – Kildare
Baile Dháith – Littleton
Cúil an tSúdaire – Portarlington

the native name
in italic print
a perverse telling of local history
the native name
in the smallest print
a faint telling becoming fainter…]

The poem's speaker is helpless: 'there are castles I will never attack/ and officials before me whose pride is great/ my own queen I'm afraid I will not defend/ I am surrounded by footsoldiers on the road.' The poem ends on a note of reluctant acceptance that it is the fate of the Irish-speaker to live athwart two cultures.

Idir dhá dháth
idir dhá fhocal
idir dhá ainm
idir dhá aigne

idir dhá áit
idir dhá theanga
a chaithim mo shaol
idir dhá shaol.

[between two colours
between two words
between two names
between two minds
between two places
between two tongues
I spend my life
between two worlds.]

Unlike Ó Searcaigh's celebration of hybridity, Breathnach presents a subject who has no choice but to accept a position of imposed hybridity. The in-between position is clearly presented as an uncomfortable and a disappointing one, an illustration of the truth of Albert Memmi's comment that 'A man straddling two cultures is rarely well-seated.' The issue becomes more problematic still when the very nature of what constitutes one's language of birth or choice is questioned.

Linguist James McCloskey, in considering the situation of Irish from the perspective of global language endangerment, had the following to say about the various forms of language which can be seen to constitute contemporary Irish:

When you think about it, the concept of Irish is a bizarre and complex construct. It includes the vernaculars of the three main Irish-speaking areas, in all the intricacy of their variations from place to place and from generation to generation; it includes the written standard in all its flexibility, with its neologisms and carefully constructed compromises among the vernaculars; it includes the rich and complex mixes of Irish and English that people in all the Gaeltacht areas experiment and play with; it includes the new urban varieties of Belfast and Dublin, created by something like the pidginization process and probably self-sustaining; it includes the even stranger mixes that are now being created by children in the Irish-speaking schools – gaelscoileanna – by the process of creolization.

Such a description of the Irish language by a professional linguist would have been unthinkable fifty years ago. It is not that people were unaware of, or uninterested in, the question of language mixing. On the contrary, ever since the beginning of the Gaelic Revival there has been a critical proccupation with the issue of linguistic purity and with protecting the language from incursions from English. Most of the discussion has focused on the work of Irish-language writers: whether they were reproducing authentic Irish, or whether they were actually writing English covered with a thin veneer of Irish. Accusations of 'Béarlachas', of the use of non-native structures, of idiom and metaphor borrowed from English, of unnatural coinings, have occurred in every generation. The existence of such Englishisms merely reflect one simple linguistic fact: that Irish has been subject for centuries to the influence of English and that its survival as a living language has occurred in a situation of active and unequal language-contact. Even those regions which came to be defined as the Gaeltacht in the 1920s were never totally monolingual. As linguist Máirtín Ó Murchú has pointed out, they are now merely the strongest end (from the point of view of Irish-language use) of a countrywide bilingual continuum.

With regard to the rest of the country, it is seldom acknowledged that the revival of Irish as a medium of communication in those areas where it had gone into disuse was inevitably going to involve a degree of 'contact-induced change'. This linguistic fact has been a bone of contention for Irish-language critics for decades, but it is only in more recent years that creative writers have begun to lift the taboos imposed on them by critics, readers and publishers, and have begun (albeit in a modest and fairly tentative manner to date) to depict actual linguistic and sociolinguistic reality. Few have dared to publish the kinds of bilingual work which a truly realist depiction of most Irish-speaking communities would demand. Problems of linguistic authenticity are often surmounted by consciously or unconsciously adopting narrative devices or generic forms which facilitate the realistic depiction of social situations through the subject position of an Irish-speaker. The success of lyric poetry in Irish, and the popularity of the autobiographical mode, can be accounted for as creative strategies to avoid the more obvious difficulties.

The concern about the kinds of Irish written and spoken has not abated, however. Ironically, such concerns have been expressed more in recent years due to the exposure given to different styles of spoken language by the expanded Irish-language broadcast media. The standard of Irish of the young broadcasters on the Dublin community radio station Raidió na Life has often been commented on; the speech styles of young presenters and actors featuring on the national television station TG4 has received negative critical attention, while even Raidió na Gaeltachta, most of whose presenters are native speakers from the Gaeltacht, has been faulted in recent years for a diminution of linguistic standards. It is as if the increased public exposure, instead of being a source of pride and pleasure, has fulfilled our worst fears: the language we love and cherish is no longer what it used to be. Of course the extent of the 'problem' is usually greatly exaggerated as salient features such as code-mixing and code-switching become central critical concerns. What is apparent, especially when young people and second-language speakers become the butt of the criticism, is a general reluctance to accept that, if the language revival had succeeded, if the majority of the people of Ireland were Irish-speakers or even active bilinguals, the Irish that they would be speaking would inevitably be a hybrid creolised version, heavily influenced by the dominant world language with which it would still be in daily contact.

Of course, the question of linguistic standards must be of concern to all those involved in language maintenance. Irish-language teachers, publishers and media organisations all have an important role to play in setting and maintaining standards. The target language for the learner of Irish should ideally be the language of the native speaker (as it would be for any other modern language). But what if it is the case that most of the language teachers are not native speakers? What if the language competence of many of these teachers is far from native-speaker standard? What if an urban Irish-language community chooses to reject the native-speaker standard, in favour of their own interlingual version? What if there is ambiguity as to the nature of native-speaker competence? Should learners be exposed to Irish in its purest forms only, to the ideal standards of a former generation, thus ignoring in the process the 'rich and complex mixes' mentioned by McCloskey in the above passage? Of course, in actuality, learners concerned with acquiring communicative competency in the language will become aware of the various styles which make up the 'complex construct' and may become competent enough to handle a range of these styles. One can also be optimistic and accept the wisdom of the creolinguist who is comfortable with the fact that 'all linguistic systems leak'; that languages are constantly changing and that such change is a sign of vitality. One can accept that interlingual forms of a language – such as '*Gaelscoilis*', or the forms of Irish spoken in Irish-speaking or bilingual households where neither parent is a native speaker – can function as successful media of communication. If the Irish language is to survive as a medium of communication, many of us may have to struggle against the prejudices associated with our own linguistic upbringing and education. We do need a more informed discussion of the linguistic processes at work when a language becomes minoritised as Irish has. It is significant that it is the creative writers, rather than the linguists, who have been to the forefront of the debate by demonstrating the tensions and challenges facing a community between two languages. For his recognition of the role of the poets, however, I will leave the last word to the linguist James McCloskey:

> It is impossible to know at this point what (if anything) will ultimately emerge from this froth of linguistic experimentation and creativity.

We can be reasonably sure that it will not much resemble anything that early revivalists such as An tAthair Peadar Ó Laoghaire would have recognised or approved of, but we can also be reasonably sure that it will be a medium in which a Cathal Ó Searcaigh or a Michael Davitt will be able to create fine and lively poetry.

The poems and excerpts quoted in this article can be found in the following publications:

Colm Breathnach, *An Fearann Breac*, Coiscéim, Dublin, 1992.
James McCloskey, *Guthanna in Éag/Voices Silenced*, Cois Life, Dublin, 2001.
Micheál Ó Conghaile, *Gnéithe d'Amhráin Chonamara ár Linne*, Cló Iar-Chonnachta, Indreabhán, 1993.
Aodh Ó Murchú, 'Dúchas na Cinniúna', *Lá*, 22 February 2001.
Cathal Ó Searcaigh, *Ag Tnúth leis an tSolas*, Cló Iar-Chonnachta, Indreabhán, 2000.

Translations of Irish-language material in the endnotes are by Máirín Nic Eoin.

Notes

1   We are thatch-cottage-ist/ and mod-con bungalo-ist,/ We are seanbhean
    bhocht-ist/ and Marilyn Monroe-ist,/ We are mean herring-ist/ and
    takeaway microwave-ist,/ We are folktale báinín-ist/ and scoopstory Sky-
    ist,/ We are visit to the well-ist/ and rock 'an roll walkman-ist,/ We are
    strong fort-ist/ and mobile home-ist,/ We are horse and cart-ist/ and
    Vauxhall Cavalier-ist,/ We are local gossip-ist/ and porn internet-ist,/ We
    are báirín breac-ist/ and pina colada cheesecake-ist,/ We are set dance-ist/
    and hokey pokey karaoke-ist./

    We are weaving our future from our past,/ Magee-ing our dirty yellow
    tweed,/ Levi-ing our corduroy trousers,/ We are weaving our future from
    our past./

2   It is a totally different Conamara we have now. Conamara of the disco, of
    rock 'n' roll, of country and western, of the walkman and the karaoke.
    Conamara of the night clubs, the potholes and the mobile homes.
    Conamara of the videos, Cablelink Conamara, Sky and satellite Conamara.
    The Conamara of 'Home and Away' and 'Coronation Street', Conamara of
    the bingo, the lotteries. Coca Cola Conamara, Conamara of the hotels and
    chippers. Conamara of the microwave, the mud wrestlers and the Sunday
    World.

    This is our Conamara, the Conamara we are sucking and breathing in each
    and every day. The Conamara that is being forced on us by world events,
    or that many of us are willingly accepting, the new Conamara that we are
    creating for ourselves. This is our culture now, not just one culture but
    cultures. At times we hardly recognise ourselves in the confusion of it all.

An Enterprise of the Spirit

Breandán Ó Doibhlin

In a recent work on the world-wide diversity of languages, Professor Roland Breton of the University of Aix-Marseille describes the linguistic situation of Ireland in the following terms:

Europe offers few examples of states which are mono-ethnic but plurilingual ... [One such is] Ireland, where the 1937 constitution recognises one national language, Irish Gaelic, the age-old speech of the island, of the Celtic family, and proclaims it as first official language, while English is only in second place. But Irish, through centuries of persecution, has steadily lost ground to English, the language of the dominant, colonising power, to such an extent that by the twentieth century the last Irish monoglots had disappeared and only a few bilingual districts survived in the most remote parts of the west. Since independence in 1922, the Irish state has continually encouraged and supported the use of its own language in the educational system and in administration. But, in spite of this definite policy, the number of bilinguals speaking Irish as well as English increased, between 1926 and 1961, only from 18% to 27%. The effort of will to keep their language alive and preserve their cultural inheritance has only partially checked the almost total linguistic absorption of the Irish. There no longer exists in Irish society a juxtaposition of two languages in two distinct linguistic spheres, but the superimposition within various strata of a single nation of two parallel forms of linguistic usage, one of which testifies to the existence of an individual and collective will for identity, and the other to the pressure of necessity within an island and an archipelago which are almost entirely English-speaking. This is an exceptional case in the spectrum of bilingualism, where the first language of the immense majority is looked on as foreign and where, as a matter of political strategy, the effort is made to propagate the ancestral tongue, at least as a second language.

The Irish reader may well wish to differ from these sentiments in points of detail or matters of emphasis, but it may be said in general that, as a statement from an objective and not unsympathetic outsider, it encapsulates the central dilemma of our language situation in this country. We have been faced for some generations now with the unpalatable fact that what Roland Breton calls 'the ancestral tongue', the language in which the vast bulk of our experience as a people is enshrined, is in considerable danger of disappearance as the expression of a living community, and this due to historical circumstances in no small degree beyond the control of our people and therefore at least partly independent of their choice. There is no need to labour the 'pressure of necessity', to use Roland Breton's phrase, which imposed and imposes the use of English upon us. To many, indeed with some of our most responsive writers in English among them, there is no longer any choice in practice and nothing more can be foreseen for Irish than as a source of cultural inspiration for the initiate, a noble heritage perhaps, but a dead language. This we must be realistic enough to envisage as a genuine possibility, maybe even a probability, and if such is to be the future, its implications for us will deserve altogether more reflection than they have been heretofore accorded.

It will, however, be conceded, I am sure, that whatever the overwhelming dominance of the English language and the likelihood of its final victory over the indigenous language, there does nevertheless exist in the country a substantial group of people who are capable, in varying degrees, of a vernacular use of Irish Gaelic and many of whom are profoundly convinced of the importance of its survival and highly motivated towards what use of it may be permitted by practical circumstances. It is this aspect of our language situation which the present essay attempts to address, since the continued existence of such elements in our population provides the only justification and the only practical basis for a discussion of this kind. It is a discussion which the protracted inadequacy of the social and political leadership of the country has unfortunately rendered of great urgency, for complacency and incomprehension have opened the way to the steady erosion of the historical constituents of our sense of ourselves.

This topic of national identity is one which has recently and quite suddenly come to the forefront of minds everywhere. It lurks constantly in the wings as the drama of European integration unfolds on stage; in its older, confrontational forms it has re-emerged after the great thaw of Marxist ideology in Eastern Europe, as Turks in Bulgaria demand to de-Slavify their names or Hungarians in Romania agitate for cultural autonomy, and minorities everywhere, whether in the ex-colonial countries of Africa or the centralised states of the European community, lay claim to the right to exist and to continue to exist. We should therefore proceed cautiously in this entire field, since there is ample evidence both from past history and current affairs that we are dealing with what quite literally can become explosive material. It is in fact this capacity for generating violent conflict that prejudices the minds of many even against any effort to raise the topic of identity at all, since it is all too easy to dismiss the whole business with the pejorative term 'nationalism', which since its use by the fascist regimes of the early part of the twentieth century became a hate-word for both the Marxist left and the liberal right. It behoves us, therefore, from the start to try to dispose of some misconceptions and to defuse the emotional tensions which untidy thinking and tactless expression so readily create.

For a start, I feel that we might avoid talking of the 'problem of the Irish language'. We live of course in an age of 'problems' when the arduous business of living tends to be presented in the form of a succession of intellectual puzzles which have to have technical solutions provided for them, much as a schoolboy used to have to turn up with answers to the geometry riders in his homework. It seems further to be assumed that discussion of these 'problems', on a public platform, or better still, on a television screen, will 'solve' them and so make life easier for all of us. It would be fairer to say that, in the present context, we are dealing with the kind of 'problem' which, in one form or another, we will always have with us, since we are close to the core of the mystery of human existence in all its ambiguity and impenetrability.

A moment's reflection will be enough to persuade us that the human condition is constituted, not of a series of 'solvable' problems so much as an endless labour of varying aspects which we slave at, or perhaps shirk, according to the degree of our energy or determination. It can also be readily seen that, whatever our energy or our determination, we are not likely to dispose of the many challenges to our existence and that we personally will cease to be, leaving to our posterity essentially the same task under ever-renewed aspects as we have had bequeathed to us. It is in this sort of spirit, it seems to me, that we should reflect on the difficulties and ambiguities, and on the vitality, of our culture – in the setting of the entire human condition and the human spirit and its paradoxes.

A personal essay on a topic of so diverse and profound a nature as this can only be a tentative thing. This is not only because any form of dogmatism or intolerance is profoundly objectionable to the contemporary mind. It is because we are in some degree or other dealing with things of the spirit. We sometimes hear it claimed these days that what the Gaelic revival movement needs is a new ideology, to replace the now threadbare ideas of the original Gaelic League. But ideologies, if by these we mean closed systems of ideas, can very easily become prisons of the spirit if they become fixed or fossilised, and fail to adapt to the incessant change around them. We must be careful, therefore, about advancing arguments of an essentialist or integrist character, and about assumptions and axioms. In any case, no intellectual process will of itself make people active in a cause. Dedication of such a kind involves every level of the personality, and it requires faith rather than ideology, a ferment rather than an orthodoxy. This, however, is not by any means to say that we cannot engage in a reasoned reflection on the mind of our society or on our historical identity and the concept we have of our past and future as a people. But, in the last analysis, an invitation to discourse on culture is an invitation to talk about life. The more rigorously it is conducted and the more in conformity with the norms and methods of logical and scientific discourse, the more it may be liable to miss the point. It is perhaps more properly the domain of the poet and novelist even than of the philosopher, and certainly than of the sociologist. The Irish language, now in its last desperate stand, may well have more need of the imagination than of technology, if only because it is easier to construct a theology than to found a faith, easier to number the dead bones than clothe them with living, new-begetting flesh. Such a discourse can only proceed from an individual, lived experience, and hope that, in its efforts to draw something of general validity from that single reflection, it may at least here and there say something of value.

In practical terms, I suppose, we are trying to decide what to do about what is, for the elites of our society, that embarrassing relic of a disreputable past, the Irish language. There it is like some toothless grandmother huddled by our hearth, mumbling over days of misery or ancient heroism that we, her forward-looking children, have never known and would sooner forget. We can't in all decency throw her out – she is after all of our blood – but we can park her in a geriatric ghetto where she can expire in comfort and in solitude, while we get on with the business of living. So we have given her government commissions to revive her, Gaeltacht grants and schemes to build up her resistance, even her own television service to cheer her last lucid hours.

To discuss her future adequately, we must be clear about some basic distinctions. We are not engaged in a discussion of political nationalism, even in its Irish version, because political nationalism will continue in Ireland irrespective of the fate of the language. Nor should we make the mistake of seeing support for the language in romantic terms, as in some sense the revival of a past Golden Age. The Gaelic League revival was marked to a considerable extent in this way by its intellectual origins in German romanticism, and its effectiveness ultimately damaged by this nostalgic pursuit of a pristine *Volksgeist*. It is hardly necessary to add that our discussion will not be helped by relying on the son of half-truths encapsulated in such traditional slogans as '*Ní tír gan teanga*' or '*Tír gan teanga, tír gan anam*' or '*Éire saor, Éire Gaelach*', just as it is superficial to put forward no better arguments in favour of the language than claiming it as a badge to distinguish us from English-speaking peoples. Apologists for the preservation of Irish would do well to keep clearly in mind the salient features of the intellectual climate in which we live. Our political context is a community of West European states, democratic and pluralist in their organisation, liberal in their philosophical outlook, confident in the universal applicability of these principles, and with a consequent cosmopolitan bias and an aversion to all forms of exaggerated nationalism.

There may very well be a considerable degree of ambiguity, hypocrisy and even contradiction in these attitudes, but they impose the terms in which our discussion must proceed. Hence, it should be made clear from the start that any argumentation in favour of support for Irish is in no sense calling into question the equality of personal philosophies or ideologies before the law. This, provided such attitudes do not endanger the peace, should go without saying. Which of course does not exclude the critical evaluation of such points of view, nor indeed a debate on the very difficult problem of reconciling the defence of minority values in practice with the principle of egalitarian pluralism. Is it sufficient, for example, to proclaim that the new Ireland must give equal place to every 'tradition' which went into its making? Again, a common emotional reaction in debates about the Irish language used to be: 'I don't speak Irish! Are you trying to make me out therefore a second class citizen?' or 'I'm just as good an Irish person as any Irish speaker!' Obviously, the personal rights of the individual citizen are not at issue and the constitution and laws of the Irish republic must be particularly jealous in 'cherishing all the children of the nation equally' – the sorry history of Northern Ireland being a permanent warning.

We are concerned rather in this debate with the more intimate and more profound regions of the national life, with what being 'children of the nation' implies for the individuals who currently wish to have their share in the existence of an Irish entity. We are trying to see more clearly into what constitutes this individuality, how it can be recognised and perhaps as a consequence to judge how such a sense of identity can be fortified and promoted, how it can be ordered by law and enshrined in institutions – a task of more than normal importance since the Irish identity was obliged to survive for long periods with practically no institutions to protect it. This latter fact is perhaps the key in the entire cultural context of contemporary Ireland, particularly in regard to the vexed questions of cultural continuity and identity.

Our history has been marked by deprivation and alienation of a type familiar to all colonised countries, but in our case of such duration and such exhaustiveness as to endanger our continued existence, and hardly matched in the experience of any other people. Ironically, it is this very experience of colonial humiliation which constitutes a major advantage of ours, whether in our relations within Europe or, as Europeans, with all those peoples who have suffered colonisation. It is a particular advantage to the Gaelic-speaker who consciously take the measure of their minority condition in their own country. For they can take comfort in the fact that theirs is a concern shared all over Europe and widely in the Third World for long-submerged or embattled cultures. There is no need to rehearse the list of languages which are springing to new life, and noticeably through the work and insight of younger people. Basque, Breton, Welsh, Occitan, Catalan, Scottish Gaelic, to take Western Europe alone, all in varying degrees show signs of renewed vitality. So far Irish has been sluggish in catching that fever, as if young people in Ireland had failed so far to appreciate that, in comparison with the above cultures, it is perhaps the weakest and most threatened of all, and perhaps too, because years of official duplicity have blinded them to the fact that they are being inexorably deprived of their birthright.

It might be apposite to interject once more at this point that the contemporary rise of minority cultures has little to do with the romantic antiquarianism of the nineteenth century. There is often in fact a clear opposition, for example in the cases of Breton and Occitan, to this traditional type of old-fashioned, patient and often pathetic loyalty. These younger movements are above all fired by the social break-up of their communities, the familiar blight of emigration, economic decline, corrupt political control, remote centralised government and the condescension of the great urban centres for what they regard as remote and backward people. The feeling would not be by any means uncommon on Ireland's western seaboard or in large areas of the provinces, but few so far have seen any connection between cultural revival and opposition to this indigenous colonialism. Unlike Ireland, these young movements have concluded that the dynamism necessary to reverse such decline cannot be generated merely by establishing the material objectives of economic progress, a truth which countries like Denmark and Finland recognised a century ago. As they would put it, they are engaged in an effort to end the alienation which a colonial-type exploitation brought upon their society, and nothing less than a rejuvenation of the whole person, the whole culture, can restore fundamental self-respect and self-reliance.

A number of such lines of argument of more or less suasive force may be pursued in the course of a reflection on the attitude to be adopted towards the Irish language. As we have been implying, the abandonment of what was one of the earliest and always a central target of the coloniser constitutes an immense historical irony for a people who have at last achieved a measure of self-determination. What such abdication implies for the moral fibre of our people in meeting other challenges to their destiny is, I should have thought, a matter of some concern. The solution of the various economic and social problems which beset us may well demand a degree of determination and self-confidence which our failure in the area of the human spirit might conclusively show us to lack. Viewed from without, the loss of what is debatably the major language and culture of the Celtic group can only be seen as a tragic impoverishment of European civilisation and the society responsible for it as deliberately relegating itself to a tributary and minor role. As the French scholar Henri Hubert wrote at a time when this country was emerging into independence: 'Something [of the Celtic languages] hung on in many places, but only as the surviving remnants of a living entity in process of erosion – that is, until the resurrection of the Irish language... It is for the Irish state to save its language.' Outsiders sometimes see more clearly than we do the absurdity which our history becomes when we reject the things that made us what we are.

Apart altogether from the need for an intelligible and adequate resolution of the issues of our past, it is no more than common sense in any consideration of our long-term cultural future to ensure that no major options are wilfully shut off. It would be difficult to over-estimate the immense wealth represented by a language and its inherent world-view, and this is doubly true of the language which was almost the sole expression of our historical experience down to the nineteenth century, the oldest cultivated European vernacular apart from Greek, and repository of an ancient, medieval and baroque civilisation which is worthy of much more attention than our educators or our artists bother to pay it. It is true too that a society which refuses to accept and exploit its own diversity is condemned in the long-term to a progressive decline in originality and in significance. And to put it at its very minimal, a Gaelic-speaking minority is entitled to the rights of a minority, that is, the realistic possibility of living its life as far as reasonably feasible through its own preferred linguistic expression, the more particularly since the continued existence of such a community is the most authentic and organic link with the long vista of our past.

Unexceptionable as these considerations may be in theory, it has to be said that their implementation in practice is very much more problematic. To put it bluntly, the Irish people have neglected their specificity to such a degree, admittedly under unprecedented extraneous pressures, that public policies of language support need to be based on the most sober assessment of aims and methods if success is to be achieved and the disillusionment of past failure to be overcome. If we reckon up the Gaelic assets that remain to us, we may count (and this is no technical essay) perhaps between five and ten per cent of our population who may be said to have a command of the language adequate for daily living. This is the demographic base on which we must work. Unfortunately this population is not grouped in any geographic or social continuum, except for the few thousand living in the scattered and remote parishes of the *fíor-Ghaeltacht*. Apart from geographic location, it is not bound together into a community by any social homogeneity, or community of economic interest, or even organs of communication. It is not really distinguished by any communal rites or gatherings like an Eisteddfod or even a Fleá Cheoil. It is in fact disparate, and submerged in the general population. No distinctive institutions mark it off, unless we cite the *naíscoil* or the *gaelscoil* or the *coláiste samhraidh*, all significantly engaged in trying to pass on the language in a society where normal family transmission has, generally speaking, disappeared.

If all this appears pessimistic, I can only repeat that a sober assessment of our situation is the only sound basis, and comforting ourselves with overstatement leads nowhere. It would seem rather that such a cold look at the situation should at once impress on us the critical urgency of whatever measures we decide upon and the fatuousness of announcing vast ambitions which have, at least for the foreseeable future, no realistic chance of success and the inevitable failure of which has only served in the past to provoke cynicism in the uncommitted, hypocrisy in the official mind, and, most seriously, discouragement in those who have worked for such aims out of idealism.

It is only fair to recall that the objectives of the revival societies of a hundred years ago, including the early Gaelic League, were the preservation and development of the Gaelic language and culture. Today, that still remains the fundamental task confronting those who interest themselves in things of the mind and spirit. And the essential minimum is the creation of some kind of vital and viable minority community whose fundamental rights can be ensured in a pluralist society, or the development of a diglossia in which Irish would have widespread acceptance as a normal mode of communication in certain areas of Irish life. Even these apparently modest aims involve overcoming major obstacles, not least that of the *de facto* objection of the population to the unsolicited use of Irish as a normal means of address. Any meaningful change in this attitude presupposes a much more accurate and honest appraisal of the part the language can play in our national well-being and the effective communication of such a vision to the public at large. This essay can do no more than offer some basic elements of a general philosophy which might help to achieve such a result.

We might preface anything we have to say with the observation that the fundamental objective of an Irish language policy must be the good estate of the people of Ireland, not the implementation of an arbitrarily established programme. Wider than the preservation or rejuvenation of a language merely, the real necessity is to establish in the country a way of life most adapted to the full development of the capacities of our people and the natural organic continuation of the identity that history has left us. In the second place, it cannot be sufficiently emphasised that it is inadequate to visualise any eventual process purely in terms of language exchange or replacement. While it is doubtful whether such a thing is possible even in theory, it is certainly of dubious worth in practice. What alone is worth the energy and sacrifice involved is a transformation of the spirit. The cynical may well dismiss such an objective as impossible idealism, but history, even our own history, provides many examples of a rejuvenation of the spirit in the lives of nations or peoples and of surges of energy which change the whole course of their affairs. And some such renewal of vitality may be needed to remedy the long-standing failure of the Irish state to resolve our economic, social and cultural difficulties. It may even be paradoxical to talk at all in terms of policies or programmes in such a context, since we are speaking in one sense or another about the ordering of the human spirit, and it is a characteristic of that spirit that its finest and most authentic manifestations cannot be programmed or produced to order. Perhaps the most we can do is to minimise obstacles to its free functioning and try cautiously and tactfully to produce a climate in which it is likely to thrive. But whatever we do or however we think, our actions and ideas must be inspired by things of the spirit and must tend consciously to promote values which we cherish as inherent to our traditions.

What a contradiction in terms it was for some over-enthusiastic revivalists (of the past, one should hope) to disparage the efforts of learners, to correct them pedantically or patronise them with their own knowledge, preaching about our native culture, while offending against one of its most admirable values, the reluctance to be hurtful to others. If a simple slogan had to be invented for revival, it should be: 'Irish – the friendly language'. It is not sufficient to replace Anglicised place-names with Gaelic forms if we do not try to restore one of the oldest and deepest traits of Gaelic culture, a sense of place, a knowledge of and attachment to the places that are important to us. Nor is the resumption of Gaelic surnames a significant achievement if unaccompanied by a sense of family tradition and some knowledge of the Gaelic world in which these names developed their significance. I would go so far as to maintain that a cultural resurgence is a moral desideratum in contemporary Ireland, in the sense that the shaping of our lives needs to proceed from those forces which maintained us in our historical development, a sense of our own uniqueness, a refusal to accept failure, a sense of continuity with our past and destiny in our future.

Some of these things may sound like mere vanity, but they are in fact the constituents and the results of an identity. The posturing of the vain is due to an inward emptiness, the lack of any genuine ambition and objective. A sense of unique individuality, on the other hand, is in a way a vital necessity, provided that it is not conceived of as superiority, something which in our world of competition and quantitative assessment is a constant temptation. In the deepest sense of the word, uniqueness of spirit belongs to and is essential to all humankind in all countries.

We have never been a great nation if being great means dominating others, founding empires and imposing one's will. But we have our own history, and one which is inferior to no other in its embodiment of the pathos and tragedy, the ambiguity and the occasional magnificence of human nature. It is the essential truths which that history teaches us that we must hold to, that we must rediscover, that we must proclaim anew by our own decisions and our own actions. It is not the critical dimension that we lack, but a certain image of ourselves and of our future, a genuine and worthwhile ambition for ourselves and our posterity. With the collapse all about us of socialist utopias, we need to hold on to the conviction that human society can be reformed and perfected. Perhaps the only effective inspiration for that conviction is simply love of country, because it is in the continuity and the progress of the society which history has made ours that the life of each and every one of us becomes part of the story of humankind. It is, then, within this overall project of the re-development of the vital forces of our people that we must consider a policy destined to find an authentic and generalised role for the Irish language in our society.

As an enterprise of the spirit, any such policy implies working, how ever indirectly, for the benefit of every area of national life; it implies a sense of responsibility for everything in the country. Hence, individuals who may be committed already to the promotion of the Irish language should realise that this cannot be achieved in isolation and that their active concern with other efforts to develop and perfect our society can help to create an atmosphere in which their primary concern is more likely to thrive. For language and community are interdependent realities and the ultimate option of our people in regard to their monolingual or bilingual status will be a decision of central importance, with profound implications for the psychological foundations of the community. Conversely, it should be pointed out that those who feel that economic development or social organisation, or any of the myriad practical concerns of modern society (from tax policies to town planning to ecology to health services to prison reform), are more realistic should reflect that the basis for tackling and resolving such problems is the human raw material of the Irish people, and that their morale and sense of purpose and direction will be of decisive importance. These in turn repose on the basic values which inspire our community, the way we see ourselves and the objectives we assign ourselves. Such values exist and are to be understood in a historical and spiritual context, which makes its own claims on the decisions we must come to concerning the role, and the fate, of a historically specific language.

Probably the most realistic thing we could do for ourselves would be to establish a sober and unsentimental assessment of where we stand. Such self-awareness is a very different thing from the self-consciousness which is so often observable in loud-mouthed defensiveness or bitter self-dismissal. It is the prelude to a matter-of-fact self-acceptance, clear-sighted about our shortcomings, but unapologetic about them as well. From such an achievement we are still far removed, if only because it presupposes an independence of mind and character which is difficult to attain in our condition as tributary and provincial canton of the vast world of English speech. To arrive at that stage, we need to re-name the world as we see it, in terms that carry forward this enterprise, and there is no reason why it cannot proceed simultaneously in both. Whether English or Irish ultimately proves the more effective medium only time will tell, but it would certainly be improvident in the extreme to commit ourselves totally to one at this juncture.

Paradoxical and unrealistic as it may seem, it may be precisely in English that this will prove impossible, so little control do we have of the cultural movement which this world language vehicles to us. Our people are about 90 per cent anglophone. The whole weight of a language of world-wide communication bears down on us every day and in every form –

not just in the communications media, but in our geographical and economic situation as well, and most intimately of all through the human impact of relationships within our own society. Yet it must be considered that there is a number of factors to dissuade us from putting all our eggs in that one basket, in spite of the fact that English is a highly-developed, versatile and apparently universal mode of communication, while Irish suffers from its long history of neglect and looks to many like the increasingly isolated survival of a now distant past. Passing over the historical ironies and emotional ambiguity which the exclusive cultivation of English would appear to leave us heir to, our somewhat parochial belief that English is in fact universally known appears to have turned us into a monoglot culture of a type which can be better afforded by richer and more powerful states than ours. The lamentable failure of our representatives to negotiate adequate official recognition for the Irish language now in fact militates against employment of our nationals in European administration and practically excludes the language from the curriculum of the European schools, while our national identity is perceived as ill-defined and lacking in depth.

However, leaving these details aside, the major inadequacy of English in serving as the single medium of our cultural life is that it is not specific to us. The hope sometimes expressed at the beginning of the twentieth century of developing a dialect of English appropriated to Irish needs has become, in the conditions of the modern world, a pipe-dream. We cannot, therefore, ever make of English the private language of the heart that can be such a bulwark and a comfort to the intimate lives of small nations with an individual expression of their own. We risk as a consequence, and because of the imbalance of forces involved, living in a permanent alienation from our own concerns and priorities, even our own deepest instincts and needs. It is of course precisely this quality of specificity which determines the importance of any particular aspect of a way of life for cultural identity. In this sense, let us say, Gaelic games contribute more to our specific identity than international games, traditional music than classical or pop music, the Irish language rather than English, at least theoretically. To be devoid of any specific characteristic betokens cultural assimilation. But what we are talking about here goes far deeper than distinguishing marks or badges of identity.

What is specific to a community is generally a legacy of its history and a witness to some kind of unifying tradition. The sense of identity so maintained is not merely a badge; it is above all an instinct for certain priorities in human life and of their importance. It is not demonstrated by a fretful drawing-away from others nor by arrogant assumptions of superiority; it precludes the mindless subordination of our attitudes and behaviour to patterns prescribed by others, but rather authorises a confident outreach, ready to learn or reject according to our own independent judgement, and it provides us with the poise and self-possession necessary for such judgement. It directs our interests amid the world's chaos, to prevent dispersion of our energies, to concentrate them for effective action, to enrich them and stimulate originality.

When it comes to talking of tradition, many of our most responsible writers acknowledge a problem of discontinuity when they write in English. Austin Clarke, Thomas Kinsella, Brian Friel, Seamus Heaney and Seamus Deane have all alluded to this question. Their solution, as articulated by Thomas Kinsella for example, would seem to be a determinist one. We are born into an English-speaking Ireland and we cannot do other than write English, make the best of it in spite of the twinges of conscience it causes us. We must forge an expression of our own in English, as indeed has been happening for at least a century in imaginative literature. Certainly this is an honorable ambition, tinged with nostalgia as it is, but strangely defeatist for writers with a regard for the potentialities of the human spirit, marked by the suspicion of a capitulation to, and the fatalistic acceptance of, a *fait accompli*. It must be said too that such a discontinuity simply interrupts any living tradition and what is being created is largely a raw, new product, with no more than a sentimental link with the Gaelic past.

It would be a mistake nonetheless, and an over-simplification, to assume that the mere replacement of English by Irish would solve at a stroke our problems of disjointed consciousness. For one thing, it is a highly unlikely eventuality in any foreseeable future and, for another, to assume that it would is to accept the same determinism that we have just spoken of. Not to mention the fact that contemporary writing in Irish so far shows little continuity with earlier Gaelic literature and in many cases is as tributary to mainstream Anglo-Saxon culture as writing in English is. Is there any hidden lesson for us in the fact that the most powerful contemporary Gaelic poet, the Scot Somhairle MacGill-Eain, is also the most profoundly imbued with tradition?

The problem, I am afraid, is not one for mechanical solutions, nor will it be resolved on the basis of essentialist and exclusivist dogmatic statements on the true nature of Irish identity. The most we can say is that English has largely been the vehicle of our battle for cultural survival since the mid-nineteenth century, but the long-term effect of committing ourselves entirely to it is to risk diminishing our specific identity and a consequent impoverishment of the creative energies which flow from it, as well as blurring and perhaps even obliterating anything but a sentimental form of historical memory. The fact remains that, if it can be recreated, a specific linguistic vehicle of identity is a powerful factor for emotional stability and psychological confidence. The cynic would say that a much more likely outcome is a continuation of our current cultural trends, a *laissez-aller* which assures us of a painless drift into a pleasant, and permanent, unconsciousness. Cultural self-possession, like that of the individual, is developed by a series of often difficult choices and by the energetic pursuit of our purposes. In the contemporary Irish situation, it means taking responsibility for our national life and its fundamental options. This is the price exacted by political autonomy.

For generations, the decisions controlling our existence were taken by another people, and our forefathers chafed under them. We now must take our own, and we must take good decisions, that is, decisions come to on the basis of our needs, our ideals and our experience. Nowhere is this truer than of our attitude to our languages, for in the case of one, circumstances have reached the last degree of urgency. To take the easy way out of self-indulgent inertia or of the irresolute acceptance of attitudes developed elsewhere from different experience would be dishonest, disreputable and ultimately self-corrupting. We must at least give informed consideration to the alternative of rejecting the slow decline of the Irish language among us. It is at least the more honourable moral option, a refusal in the name of human dignity and freedom to acquiesce in the ravishment of the past, however quixotic that may initally appear.

We can be sure of being in the direct line of the dynamic of our history as a people ever since the process of colonisation and assimilation was launched in this country. In such a context, a reasoned and effective policy aimed at finding an energising role for the Irish language in the life of our national community must surely be worth the effort involved in thinking it out, in mustering all those forces which are opposed to death, the death of abdication, of consumerism and alienation, of conformism and ultimate assimilation. It will be our effort to make a new contribution to humanity by evolving an identity and imagining a moral project in continuity with what we believe the past has made us, and tending resolutely to future fulfilment.

From Language Revival to Language Survival

Donncha Ó hEallaithe

Introduction

The Irish State, established in 1922 with a native government at the helm, adopted the revival of Irish as an important national objective. This was to be expected as the state was born out of a struggle for independence, the ideological basis for which was dependent to a large extent on asserting a separate national identity based on language. It was hoped that Irish would replace English in the same way as English had replaced Irish in the previous century. This was to be accomplished by teaching Irish to all schoolchildren, and by making Irish compulsory for all state examinations and for entry into the civil service. It was intended to Gaelicise the internal work of the administration as soon as sufficient civil servants had a working ability in the language. It was also hoped that the language shift in the Gaeltacht could be reversed, so that new territories could be added to the existing Irish-speaking areas.

Up to the 1960s the state more or less continued to insist on reviving Irish, even though the results of efforts in the previous forty years were disappointing. While many people had been taught Irish, there was little opportunity to use it outside of school. The Irish-speaking areas continued to shrink, although at a slower rate. The burden of reviving Irish was causing resentment and whatever public enthusiasm for revival that may have existed during the 1920s and 1930s had evaporated by the

1960s. This lead to changes in policies which fuelled a feeling of betrayal among Irish-language enthusiasts as the state retreated from revival to a vague form of language promotion.

What went wrong with the revival? Was it ever feasible? Would the pursuit by the state of more realisable linguistic objectives have yielded better results? What are the chances of Irish surviving as a living language, or will it become another of the thousands of languages that will become extinct during this century? These are some of the issues that will be looked at in this review of the Irish revival project.

The Initial Success of the Revival Movement

Some of the earliest protagonists for Irish were not revivalists at all. Douglas Hyde, a founder of the Gaelic League, seemed to acknowledge the impossibility of reviving Irish in a paper published in 1886.

> There is no use in arguing the advantage of making Irish the language of our newspapers and clubs, because that is and ever shall be an impossibility; but for several reasons we wish to arrest the language in its downward path, and if we cannot spread it (as I do not believe we very much can), we will at least prevent it from dying out and make sure that those who speak it now, will also transmit it unmodified to their descendants.[1]

However, with Hyde's later call for the 'de-Anglicisation' of Ireland and the subsequent growth of the 'Irish-Ireland' movement, of which the Gaelic League under Hyde's leadership was a key component, there was an ideological shift from preservation towards the notion that Irish could replace English.[2] Just as the GAA was attempting with some success to replace 'foreign games' with Gaelic sports, it was felt that English should be replaced by Irish as the common language of the Gael. The Irish-Irelanders of the Gaelic League saw their task as one of building a cultural exclusivity, which banned all things 'foreign'. Some of the more extreme members even regarded the wearing of trousers as suspect and took to wearing kilts.

The initial success of the Gaelic League in the pre-independence era was astounding. In 1900 the Irish language was accepted as a mainstream optional subject within the British national school system, to be taught during school hours. By 1906 it was accepted as a suitable medium of instruction in Gaeltacht schools. The most extraordinary victory of all was the vote in 1913 by the Senate of the newly-established National University of Ireland that Irish would be compulsory for entrants to all colleges of the NUI, a regulation that holds to this day.

These important and impressive improvements in the status of Irish in the educational system increased the number of Irish-speakers outside the Gaeltacht, but had little or no effect on the position of Irish among the impoverished Irish-speaking areas on the western seaboard. The 1911 census of population recorded a decline during the previous decade in the number of Irish-speakers in all provinces within Gaeltacht areas. In Leinster, the only province without a Gaeltacht area, there was a significant increase in the percentage of Irish speakers from 1.2 per cent in 1891 to 3.5 per cent in 1911. The rate of increase of Irish-speakers in Leinster accelerated between 1911 and 1925, due in no small measure to the increased educational status of the language as well as a heightened sense of patriotic fervour during the struggle for independence. The revival movement, it seems, was having a significant impact in English-speaking areas of the country, but was, at best, only slowing down the disappearance of Irish in the Irish-speaking areas and was certainly not arresting it (see Table 1).[3]

Table 1:

Number of Irish speakers by province. In brackets: percentage of Irish speakers in population.

Year	Leinster	Munster	Connacht	Ulster (part of)
1881	27,252 (2.2%)	445,766 (33.5%)	366,191 (44.6%)	85,372 (19.5%)
1891	13,677 (1.2%)	307,633 (26.2%)	274,783 (37.9%)	68,294 (17.8%)
1901	26,436 (2.3%)	276,268 (25.7%)	245,580 (38.0%)	71,426 (20.7%)
1911	40,225 (3.5%)	228,694 (22.1%)	217,087 (35.5%)	67,711 (20.5%)
1926	101,474 (8.8%)	198,221 (20.4%)	175,209 (31.7%)	68,607 (22.9%)

Source of Data: Census 1996, Volume 9

This did not escape the notice of Séamas Ó hAodha[4], who in February 1914 advocated a major change of tack for the Gaelic League in an article entitled 'The Language – A New Policy' in which he wrote the following:

> If the Gaelic League made it its business to enable the Gael to live in the Gaeltacht and prosper there, and dropped all its other work, the language would be saved. If the League continues to do everything else but this, the language will be lost.[5]

He went on to suggest in his article that the headquarters of the Gaelic League be transferred 'from the centre of Anglicisation' to the 'Gaelic-speaking fringe', meaning Galway. Hughes criticised the Gaelic League for its emphasis on Gaelicising the country through the educational system, while the living language was disappearing through emigration from the Irish-speaking areas. He wanted the Gaelic revival to be proactive in the development of Irish-speaking industry in the Gaeltacht. As he saw it the revival movement was more interested in gaining support among the urban middle class, rather than depending on the illiterate raggle-taggle of uncouth native Irish-speakers, who would first have to become English-speakers before the Gaelic revival, as such, would have any relevance for them. To the best of my knowledge Séamas Ó hAodha was the first person within the Gaelic League to question the wisdom of the devoting of its energies to reviving Irish in the Anglicised areas, but he got little support for his ideas.

The Revival Post-Independence

A language which was nothing more than an ornament to a race never survived and never will survive.

Pádraig Ó Conaire

The Executive of the Cosgrave Free State government had many committed Gaelic Leaguers in the Cabinet who believed that a native government would carry forward the project of the revival to a successful conclusion.[6] A three-pronged attack was launched, each meeting with limited success:

1. The first Minister for Education was the formidable founder of the Gaelic League, Eoin Mac Néill, who set about the Gaelicisation of the educational system.[7] Logically enough he started with the primary schools, but was soon complaining in government memos that all the efforts at Gaelicisation through the educational system 'will be wasted if the other Departments do not co-operate in keeping them Gaelicised when they leave school.' The lack of qualified teachers in Irish at primary level meant that Government directives on the use of Irish as a medium of instruction could only be partially enforced.[8]
2. The Minister for Finance, Ernest Blythe, spearheaded the Gaelicisation of the work of the Civil Service, but met with internal resistance within his own Department.[9]
3. Richard Mulcahy chaired Coimisiún na Gaeltachta, which was set up by the Cosgrave government in 1925. Within sixteen months of work, it managed to hear evidence around the country about the state of the Gaeltacht. It organised a

linguistic census of areas which had recorded a significant number of Irish-speakers in the 1911 Census and it then drew up the boundaries for both the *fíor-Ghaeltacht* (areas where over 80 per cent of the population were Irish-speaking) and *breac-Ghaeltacht* (areas where from over 25 per cent to 79 per cent of the population were Irish-speaking).[10]

So while the state seemed to be serious in its attempt at language revival, popular enthusiasm for the idea was lagging a long way behind. Support for the symbolic use of Irish as an ornamental embellishment of state was very high, but it is not clear that there was a groundswell of support for replacement of English by Irish.[11] There is no evidence that the English-speaking parts of the country had any desire to change language. It must be remembered that the new state, which emerged from the national struggle, retained the same administrative procedures and practices as well as essentially the same personnel as the British administration. So the state apparatus inherited by the Free State could not be accused of being enthusiastic for the Gaelicisation of the civil service.

On the education front, concern was being expressed that the emphasis on Irish in primary schools and the use of Irish as a medium of instruction in English-speaking areas was having a detrimental effect on the quality of education received by schoolchildren. This was acknowledged politically at the time, but was seen as a necessary and acceptable price to pay. Naturally enough, what initial enthusiasm existed for the language among the wider public turned to apathy, or even antagonism, when it began to emerge that the quality of children's education may have been suffering owing to the emphasis on Irish.[12]

... calls for an investigation into the effect the policy was having on the attainment of children, the quality of education being received and the position and status of the language were ignored. Such calls were partly deflected through efforts to discredit critics of the policy. ... The failure to carry out any scientific analysis into the level of success of the policy, or the effect it was having on the curriculum and the standard of education, despite contemporary calls to do so, perhaps betrayed an unease that such an investigation would have resulted in a negative evaluation ... [13]

It is fair to say that during the post-independence era, dominated as it was by the towering figure of de Valera on the one hand and the pre-Vatican II Catholic Church on the other, the Irish-Ireland project became a disturbing retreat into a conservative type of cultural protectionism. The Catholic Church, which more or less shaped the pervasive ideology of the new state, saw this cultural protectionism as a guard against the twin evils of sexual immorality on the one hand and dangerous secular ideas like socialism and atheistic communism on the other. In those years the Gaelic League seemed to attract to its ranks people who subscribed to this conservative ideology and at the same time succeeded in alienating a whole generation of post-independence intellectuals, who might have backed a less conservative and more pluralist type of cultural agenda.[14] The Gaelicising project lost an important ally in Ireland when the intellectuals turned their backs. Their indifference at best, or hostility at worst, allowed the language project to rot in its own contradictions.

The Policy of Compulsory Irish is Challenged

The 1960s was a pivotal decade for the new state. Previous assumptions were questioned and policies were jettisoned. The state's policy on the Irish language came under intense scrutiny from both sides of the argument. On the one hand, Irish-language organisations and activists were displaying a growing impatience and frustration at the lack of progress by the state in advancing the revival. On the other hand the policy of compulsory Irish had become a highly contentious and emotive issue.[15] During the 1961 election campaign Fine Gael called for an end to the policy of compulsory Irish in state examinations. The Irish-language movement, which still had considerable clout in the mid-sixties, responded with a national petition in 1964, entitled 'Let the Language Live'. It was successful in gathering hundreds of thousands of signatures and came at an appropriate time, as the Government was preparing a White Paper which would detail its policy on the issue of language revival.[16]

The White Paper, entitled 'The Restoration of the Irish Language' (1965), reiterated that Government policy with regard to the Irish language was 'to restore the Irish language as a general medium of communication.' It also appeared to reaffirm the Government's commitment to compulsory Irish in state examinations. However, on compulsory Irish in the civil service, it signalled that it might reconsider 'whether the absolute preference for competence in Irish should not be replaced by a system of merely awarding marks proportionate to the candidate's knowledge of Irish'.

By the mid-sixties, the question of compulsory Irish had become one of the great emotive issues of the decade, fuelled by impassioned encounters on *The Late Late Show* which, under the baton of Gay Byrne, had become compulsive viewing for the entire nation every Saturday night. The newly-formed Language Freedom Movement (LFM) was engaged in a campaign for a change in state policy. It succeeded in attracting to it ranks the prolific Irish-language writer Séamus Ó Grianna from the Donegal Gaeltacht and the Kerry writer John B. Keane, but the bulk of the membership consisted of people who resented having to learn Irish in order to pass the Leaving Certificate examination or to be eligible for a job or promotion in the civil service, or to gain entry to the only universities in the state which Catholics were allowed by their Church to attend.[17]

It was hard to put forward a reasonable defence in favour of Irish being the only compulsory subject in state examinations, considering that a failure in Irish in the Leaving Certificate disqualified a person from most careers in the public service, and a failure in Irish in the Group Certificate examination ruled out opportunities for children from poorer backgrounds to rise above the lowest rung of social stratification reserved for the unskilled.[18]

Passions boiled over at a public meeting on 21 September 1966, organised in the Mansion House by the LFM. The Irish-language movement mobilised its forces.

About 2,000 people turned up and jammed into every available space in the room. It was clear that the overwhelming majority of them were unfriendly towards the organisers of the meeting. There was enough shouting, jeering, heckling, booing and chanting to drown out the chairman's opening remarks. Union Jacks were waved derisively at the platform. On the platform itself was an Irish tricolour, which a member of the audience made haste to seize at the outset, shouting that the national flag should not be displayed at a meeting of this kind. As he was hustled away a shower of papers was flung at the stage and a stink bomb was let off. Immediately after this a fight broke out, involving about ten men. It was evident there was going to be serious trouble unless something was done to lower the temperature.[19]

The meeting was only allowed to proceed when the LFM agreed to hear four speakers in favour of Irish, in order to restore some degree of calm to the proceedings.[20] The Irish-language organisations on the night may have considered that the Mansion House challenge to the LFM was a victory – and it may have felt like that in the heat of the moment – but attempting to deal with the legitimate issues raised by the LFM by breaking up meetings was not going to make the emotive issue of compulsory Irish go away.

A more strategic response might have yielded better results in the medium to long term. However, Irish-language organisations were ideologically attached to the notion of the restoration of Irish as the vernacular of the country. The leading activists had restored Irish in their own lives and thought everybody else should do the same. They went for broke in the 1960s on the issue of compulsory Irish and lost almost everything in the 1970s.

The Abandonment of the Revival by the State

It was officially admitted by the Commission on the Restoration of the Irish Language that little progress was being made in reviving Irish. One of the obstacles identified was the emphasis in schools on written language rather than the spoken tongue. To tackle this problem the Franciscan priest, Colmán Ó Huallacháin, developed a revolutionary audio-visual course for primary schools called *Buntús Cainte*, which was launched with great fanfare in 1966. He also lobbied for the setting up of a linguistics research institute, so as to help the language project to make progress using trained people, rather than relying on what he called 'amateur common sense'. The Minister for Education, Donough O'Malley, duly complied and in 1967 set up Institiúid Teangeolaíochta Éireann to provide expert advice on the revival effort.[21]

Colmán Ó Huallacháin was appointed as Director. A fine spacious office was secured on Fitzwilliam Street in Dublin, but after four years senior staff appointments had still not been made and no research projects could begin. The Department of Education frustrated all attempts at initialising the recruitment process.[22] In the end Colmán Ó Huallacháin wrote in exasperation to the international expert Dr Joshua Fishman, who had been involved in advising the Government on the setting up of ITÉ. Fishman's reply is worth noting:

... during the past decade I have been consultant on language matters to a dozen governments, most of my recommendations have been accepted ... some rejected recommendations that were not to their liking ... what does disturb me is the now quite apparent delaying tactics whereby recommendations are neither rejected nor implemented but simply surrounded by administrative silence and inaction ... after four years, I have come to the conclusion that I have been used not as a consultant but as an unwitting participant in a master plan to do nothing ... I have lately concluded that this is exactly what the Irish Government wants.[23]

Ó Huallacháin went public about the deliberate stalling and in April 1971 was told his services were no longer required.

In the 1973 election campaign, Labour and Fine Gael promised that in government they would end compulsory Irish in state examinations and the Irish requirement for entry to the civil service.[24] In office they were as good as their word. Soon after his appoinment, the Coalition's new Irish-speaking Minister for Education, Richard Burke, announced at a press conference the termination of the requirement to pass Irish in order to pass state examinations. He successfully ingratiated himself with language activists by reopening Scoil Dhún Chaoin as a shrewd gesture of goodwill.[25]

When it was announced, a few months after the election, that a pass in Irish would no longer be compulsory in state examinations there was little or no opposition to the measure. It was also announced that an honours grade in Irish was to be henceforth worth two honours for the Higher Education Grant.[26] The subsidy paid to Gaeltacht households by the Government for keeping students attending Irish colleges was to be doubled. The Irish-language lobby was effectively bought off by these few 'sweeteners', which were offered in appeasement.[27]

The Language Freedom Movement's campaign was yielding results. The other main target of its campaign was the requirement to pass an Irish test for entry to the civil service. In November 1974 the Coalition Government announced new language requirements for entrants to the civil service, which effectively abolished the requirement to pass an exam in Irish. Fianna Fáil's George Colley closely questioned the Minister responsible, Richard Ryan, and in the Dáil said that Fianna Fáil would restore Irish as a requirement for entry to the civil service when it would next form a government – but they didn't.

On returning to government with a landslide in 1977, Fianna Fáil was quite happy to leave things as they were. This must register as one of the great failures of the Irish-language movement in the modern era. It could have argued for a compromise solution and might therefore have succeeded in convincing Fianna Fáil of the merits of having a proper Irish-language requirement for a high proportion of the jobs in the civil service and in local government, so that the state would be in a position to fulfil at least its constitutional obligations with respect to providing a service in Irish for people in the Gaeltacht and for Irish-speakers in general.

The Irish-language movement has not been good at seeking a strategic compromise. It still isn't. The 'all or nothing approach' generally results in nothing in the long run. In the 1970s recruitment policy in the civil service went from a position where Irish was compulsory for everybody to Irish being compulsory for nobody. A consequence of three decades of this policy is that it will be very difficult for a lot of state agencies to comply with the provisions of the Official Languages Act 2003. Having sufficient people on the staff who can offer a service to Irish-speakers is now governed by the laws of probability rather than recruitment criteria.

The failure of the Lynch Government of 1977 to fulfil its promise to reverse the removal by the previous Government of the Irish-language requirement for entry to the civil service marks the official abandonment by the state of the revival/restoration project. While blocking people from passing a state examination because they failed Irish could not be defended, a requirement that a high proportion of jobs in the public service be reserved for people with a proven ability to speak and write Irish would seem not only reasonable but a constitutional imperative.

A constitutional imperative ignored by the state from 1980 onwards was the provision of Acts of the Oireachtas in both languages. Adrian Hardiman, in a scathing judgement delivered in the Supreme Court in April 2001, found the state in 'clear and obvious breach' of Article 25.4.4 of the constitution.[28] He went on to say:

> In my view ... [the State breach of the Constitutional requirement] has led to a situation where only a person of unusual independence of mind and pertinacity will attempt to conduct his or her legal business through the medium of Irish. If such a person seeks a statute in Irish from the official Government outlet he or she is more than likely to be told it is not available. There is no Irish version of the forms required to institute a simple claim in Irish in the District Court, nor of the forms to enable a person, for example, to summon a witness or commence an appeal... only litigation or the threat of litigation will produce these documents. This state of affairs is a constant officially tolerated discouragement or actual preclusion from the conduct of legal business in the national language... I can only say that this situation is an offence to the letter and spirit of the constitution.

That a citizen wishing to do business in Irish with the state could only manage to do so by taking legal action is a massive indictment of successive governments, and is an indictment also of the great movement founded by Douglas Hyde and Eoin Mac

Néill in that it failed to provide any worthwhile challenge as the state deliberately reneged on its constitutional obligations, leaving the legal battles to individual activists at the risk of great personal cost to themselves.

While the Irish-language movement may have won the battle of the Mansion House back in 1966, by 1980 they had well and truly lost the war. Official Ireland had abandoned the revival in favour of a rather vague form of bilingualism, which was being promoted on behalf of the state by the newly established Bord na Gaeilge. This form of bilingualism was never defined and never managed to extend as far as the provision of services in both official languages, even in the Gaeltacht. It was a far cry from the wishful thinking at government level that seemed to believe it might be possible to gradually replace English by Irish throughout the country.

Efforts to Halt Language Shift in the Gaeltacht

Cumann na nGaedheal, which formed the first post-independence government, viewed the saving of the Gaeltacht as a constituent part of the larger language revival strategy and in that context set up Coimisiún na Gaeltachta in 1925.[29] The Commission was given the task of (i) laying out the boundaries of Irish-speaking and partly Irish-speaking districts; (ii) making recommendations as to the use of Irish in the administration of such districts and the educational facilities needed; (iii) recommending steps that should be taken to improve the economic conditions of the inhabitants.

The work undertaken by the 1926 Commission is very impressive, considering the times that were in it. In hindsight it is fair to say that the 1926 Commission seriously overestimated the actual extent of the Gaeltacht and seriously underestimated the task of maintaining Irish as the main language of communication in existing Gaeltacht communities.

That said, however, if the practical recommendations of the Commission had been acted on, the decline of the Gaeltacht, as illustrated in the table below, may actually have been halted, whatever about being reversed.

Table 2: Ability to speak Irish in the *fíor-Ghaeltacht*

Year	Total Population	Irish Speakers	% Irish Speakers in Gaeltacht	% Irish Speakers in State
1911*	189,755	149,677	79%	17.6%
1926	164,774	146,821	89%	18.3%
1936	148,218	123,125	83%	23.7%
1946	137,207	104,941	76%	21.2%
1961†	79,323	64,275	81%	27.2%
1971	70,568	55,440	79%	28.3%
1981	79,502	58,026	73%	31.6%
1991	83,286	56,469	65%	32.5%
2002	86,517	62,157	73%	42.8%

* These figures are for the areas which were subsequently recognised as *fíor-Ghaeltachtaí* in 1926.

† These figures are for the reduced Gaeltacht area, defined by a redrawing of the boundaries in 1956.
Source: Various Census Reports

The majority of Irish-language enthusiasts never properly acknowledged how it must have felt for Gaeltacht people who had little command of English. A man from Aran, giving evidence to Coimisiún na Gaeltachta in 1926 had this to say: 'It is only them with plenty of English who are bothered about Irish.' Despite the highest status being accorded to the Irish language in the Free State constitution and later in *Bunreacht na hÉireann*, Gaeltacht people without an acceptable fluency in English were effectively second-class citizens in their own country, when it came to dealing with the wider society or seeking services from the state for themselves and their children.[30]

To compound the problem, it is estimated that as many as two out of every three native Irish-speakers, many with a poor command of English, were forced to leave the Gaeltacht for England or America during the 1950s. Approximately 10,000 left the Conamara Gaeltacht in the years 1946 to 1966. Not only did this result in a sharp drop in the population and a distortion in the age structure, but having to emigrate to London or to Boston or even to Dublin with inadequate English made an indelible impression on the minds of those young men and women. They had been let down by an educational system which failed to equip them with sufficient English for them to feel comfortable outside the Gaeltacht. Despite all the rhetoric about Gaelicising the whole country and Irish being the first official language of the state, there were few opportunites available to the native Irish-speaker from Conamara or from West Kerry or from North-West Donegal, unless they could speak English with the fluency of a native English-speaker.[31] It is little wonder that that so many Gaeltacht people with poor English decided that they should speak whatever bit of English they had to their children before they went to school and let the schools teach them Irish. Wasn't that what most of the shopkeepers and the school teachers did in the Gaeltacht?

Saving the Gaeltacht through Industrialisation

The Department of the Gaeltacht was established in 1956 by the 1953-57 Coalition Government and the Mayo TD Patrick Lindsay was appointed Parliamentary Secretary for the Gaeltacht. Lindsay's main achievement in a very short period of office was to redraw the boundaries of the Gaeltacht. Like any politician left with such a sensitive task, he extended the Gaeltacht boundary of his own constituency of Mayo, but excluded all the areas in de Valera's constituency of County Clare.[32] If the shoe was on the other foot, I'm sure de Valera would not have been found wanting in keeping large chunks of his constituency in the Gaeltacht. The poisoned chalice of a long overdue redrawing of the boundaries now falls to Éamon Ó Cuív.

Even though the 1956 boundaries were closer to the reality, they were still based on language knowledge rather than language use. Pádraig Ó Riagáin, one of the foremost and most experienced experts in the area of sociolinguistic research, has stated that most of the areas which were excluded from the Gaeltacht in the 1956 revision had been actually English-speaking in 1926.[33]

By the mid-fifties the population of the Gaeltacht was dropping rapidly. The problems were obvious. Around 75 per cent of the workforce was engaged in subsistence farming, which could only provide a limited income and a poor living. Long established patterns of emigration were rapidly bleeding off the young people. It was perceived at the time that the solution to the problems of the Gaeltacht lay in the provision of employment at home, in order to stem emigration. To this end, in 1957 Gaeltarra Éireann was established, with its Head Office in Dublin.

Gaeltarra Éireann was given the twin duties of setting up schemes of employment and helping with the preservation of Irish as an everyday language in the Gaeltacht. It was assumed that if the rapid decline in the population of the Gaeltacht could be arrested through providing jobs at home for native Irish-speakers, then the Gaeltacht could be saved. A decentralised re-energised Gaeltarra Éireann, under the dynamic leadership of Cathal Mac Gabhann, set about attracting industries to the Gaeltacht. Industrial Estates were built, land banks were established and industrialists were encouraged to locate in the Gaeltacht. While there were failures, the overall results are impressive.[34] Jobs were provided which allowed emigrants to come home and eventually turn the population decline around in most Gaeltacht areas, but not without cost to the language.

Sociolinguists such as Hilary Tovey, Pádraig Ó Riagáin and Máirtín Ó Murchú have all drawn attention to the detrimental effect industrialisation was having on the position of Irish in the Gaeltacht.

> Ironically, efforts by central government to maintain the viability of the Gaeltacht population through a programme of industrialisation have increased the tendency towards language shift and have put the survival of the distinctive Gaeltacht communities in even greater jeopardy. As Ireland's industrialisation expended in the 1960s and 1970s, the Gaeltacht industrial authority, Gaeltarra Éireann and its successor Udarás na Gaeltachta, introduced modern industry to Gaeltacht areas. The intention, admirable in itself, was to bring increased employment to the Gaeltacht, improve the standard of living there, and stem the flow of emigration. Frequently new plants were out of scale with the local availability of manpower and a proportion of the workforce had to be recruited from outside the Gaeltacht, or Gaeltacht emigrants were induced to return and brought with them English-speaking families. In any case higher and more specialist skills had, of necessity, to be sought elsewhere.[35]

However, providing jobs became almost the sole *raison d'etre* of Gaeltarra Éireann and its successor Údarás na Gaeltachta.[36] The statutory duty of 'preservation and extension of the use of Irish as a vernacular language in the Gaeltacht' was not allowed to get in the way of employment provision, even where such provision was detrimental to the language. A *laissez-faire* attitude was adopted on the question of the effects of industrialisation on the linguistic situation. Linguistic conditions, if attached to grant applications, were not monitored. Grant-aided industries were given a free hand in recruitment, with the result that a significant proportion of jobs created were filled by non Irish-speakers, even in Irish-speaking areas of the Gaeltacht.[37] Many of the Údarás-sponsored workplaces eventually become English-language dominated environments, even in the strongest Irish-speaking communities, such as An Cheathrú Rua in South Conamara or in Gaoth Dobhair in North-West Donegal. Industrialisation was allowed to take place without any proper monitoring or evaluation of its effects on the linguistic balance of Irish-speaking communities.

A welcome shift in policy can be detected in recent years, partly driven by the Minister for the Gaeltacht, Éamon Ó Cuív, who is demanding more spending by the Údarás on language maintenance and partly by the drying-up of industrial investment in low-skilled jobs, as these jobs locate to cheaper labour locations abroad. While it should be acknowledged that Údarás na Gaeltachta seems to be in the process of reconsidering its strategies, it has to be said that a lot of irreparable damage has been inflicted on the everyday use of Irish within some of the stronger Gaeltacht communities over the last thirty years of industrialisation.

What Went Wrong?

Policy for about two decades has clearly been to let the language die by stealth.

J.J. Lee (1989)

The revival failed, in my opinion, because it was an aspiration rather than a realistic objective. Neither the Cumann na nGaedheal Government under W.T. Cosgrave (1923-1932) nor the Fianna Fáil Government under de Valera (1932-1948), can be blamed for any lack of commitment. There were errors in strategy and there was a fundamental misunderstanding of the complicated process of language change. The basic problem was the lack of public support for the unrealistic objective of replacing English with Irish.

In the final chapter of his book *Ireland 1912-1985*[38] the eminent historian J.J. Lee describes the public attitude towards the language as 'inertly benign'. He castigates the Department of Education for lacking 'the intellectual calibre to conceptualise the challenge correctly' and goes on to say that 'the official mind was blinkered by the view that just as the schools had allegedly killed the language in the nineteenth century, so they could revive it in the twentieth'. He contends that compulsory Irish was discredited because the state, having insisted on people knowing Irish, did not provide opportunities for its use.

> The charade of Irish language tests for public employment when everyone knew the language would hardly ever be used again, the whole fetid system of favouritism associated with language knowledge, as distinct from language use, inevitably left its mark, stamping the most idealistic and most important task undertaken by the new state as yet one more sleazy political racket.

He says that the state tried to revive Irish from the bottom up instead of from the top down: 'The challenge for the politicians and the administrators was not to compel children to learn to read or write Irish. It was to read and write it, and above all, to speak it themselves.'

Whatever angle one takes, it has to be admitted that the revival of the Irish language has been a failure. The preliminary report of the 2002 Census shows that out of a million adults who claim to be able to speak Irish, only 73,000 (2.6 per cent of the adult population) claim to use it on a daily basis, of which 21,000 live within the boundaries of the Gaeltacht. The table below gives the details, with figures in brackets showing the results from the 1996 Census.

Table 3
Extent of the use of Irish on a daily basis

	Gaeltacht	Non-Gaeltacht	Total
Pop. of 3-4 yrs old	2,453	108,969	111,422
Use Irish Daily (3-4 yr)	903 (861)	5,088 (3,951)	5,991 (4,812)
% Daily Users (3-4 yr)	36.8% (34.4%)	4.7% (3.6%)	5.4% (4.6%)
Population >19 yrs	62,888	2,713,699	2,776,587
Use Irish Daily (> 19 yrs)	20,723 (20,813)	52,111 (50,137)	72,834 (70,950)
% Daily Users (> 19 yrs)	33% (37%)	1.9% (2.1%)	2.6% (2.9%)

Source of Data: Census 1996 and Census 2002.

While the educational system has given an ability in Irish to approximately two out of every five adults, very few of them use it to any significant extent. There is evidence from the Census of a growing number of three- to four-year-old pre-school children using Irish.[39] This is probably due to a combination of the influence of TG4 since 1996 and the growing demand for places in *gaelscoileanna*.

Taking Stock

If we are to take stock of the use of Irish in the areas designated as *Gaeltachtaí*, it appears that approximately 20,000 people live in bilingual communities in which Irish is still the dominant language among most age groups in the home and in the community and in which English is a secondary language.[40] These concentrations of Irish-speakers are located in North-West Donegal, centred around Gaoth Dobhair with a population of 6,000 people, South Conamara from An Spidéal to Carna with a population of 10,000, the Aran Islands with a population of 1,500 people and Iarthar Dhuibhneach with a population of 2,000 people.

There are other Gaeltacht pockets in which a significant minority of adults use Irish in the home and in the community and in which Irish is used widely as a cultural medium and a medium for education. The areas that spring to mind are Ráth Cairn (Meath), An Rinn (West Waterford), Cúil Aodha (Cork), An

Ghaeltacht Láir (Donegal), Ceathrú Thaidhg and Eachléim (North-West Mayo), Na Forbacha and Corr na Móna (North Conamara), and Árainn Mhór to a lesser extent. There is something special that is worth preserving in these communities and they deserve to be designated as *breac-Ghaeltacht* areas.

However, it should be noted that even in the strongest Gaeltacht communities, English seems to be replacing Irish as the primary language among teenagers and younger adults, which does not bode well for the future. In some of the strongest Irish-speaking areas of the Gaeltacht, the proportion of homes in which Irish is transmitted may not be enough to ensure the position of Irish as the main community language. Good sociolinguistic strategies are needed to preserve the linguistic balance in the remaining Irish-speaking communities.

The last ten years have seen some other important developments, all of which should have a positive impact on the use of the Irish language by those who profess to be able to speak it:

- The success of TG4, set up in 1996 as a TV channel to serve *'pobal na Gaeilge agus na Gaeltachta'*;
- The new information available in Census returns with regard to the extent to which Irish is actually used by people allows for regular monitoring;
- The recognition for the first time in the Planning and Development Act 2000 that planning authorities have a statutory duty to 'protect the linguistic and cultural heritage of the Gaeltacht' when formulating five-year development plans;
- The recognition of the duties of Gaeltacht schools in the Education Act and the establishment of a special unit to deal with language issues;
- The Official Language Act 2003 and the appointment of The Official Languages Commissioner;
- The recently announced €500,000 linguistic study into the situation of Irish in the Gaeltacht;

- The phenomenal growth of *gaelscoileanna* and *gaelcholáistí* around the country;
- The development of An Chultúrlann as a vibrant Irish-language cultural centre in the heart of West Belfast, which provides a wonderfully attractive focal point for the Irish-speaking community of that city;
- The growth in attendance of young Irish-speakers at the annual Oireachtas Irish-language festival;
- The success of the new Irish-language newspapers *Foinse* and *Lá*;
- The setting up of four-year degree programmes, taught through Irish, both in DCU and in GMIT, and the commitment of NUIG to develop a range of degree programmes through Irish in the future;
- The development in Ireland of a multicultural society which makes it more acceptable to be heard speaking Irish;
- The vibrancy of the most Irish-speaking parts of the Gaeltacht, which are no longer shedding their young people. An expression of the new sense of confidence is the winning of senior county football finals in recent years by Gaoth Dobhair (Donegal), An Cheathrú Rua (Galway) and An Ghaeltacht (Kerry);
- The continued loyalty to Raidió na Gaeltachta of Gaeltacht people, who regard it as the community radio station.

Conclusion

> *An infallible way to paralyse people is to aim at a utopia.*
> D. P. Moran

While the Irish language is an accepted national symbol of great importance and a defining badge of identity, the primary function of every living language is to be an effective everyday means of communication for people. At present, Irish as an everyday means of communication is seldom heard outside the Gaeltacht. Within the Gaeltacht its use is diminishing and it seems that the language itself as an effective tool for communication among young people is being rejected, although data is not available on the language behaviour of teenagers and young adults.

While the official status of the Irish language at the beginning of the twenty-first century is a bit like the position of the worker in the former Soviet Union – high in theory but very low in practice – all is not lost. The retreat of the state from the official policy of reviving or restoring Irish has opened the door to the more realisable project of language maintainance, not just in the Gaeltacht but within minority networks of Irish speakers who wish to use Irish in the family home, at work, at play, for cultural expression and for socialising.

The problem with the Irish-language movement is that it still hangs on to the utopian aim of restoration. The latest example of the Irish-language movement's propensity for the pursuit of wild dreams is the Stádas campaign for recognition of Irish as a working language within the EU, in the vague hope that a status in the corridors of Brussels denied it in the corridors of Merrion Street might save the Irish language from extinction.

It is too easy to blame the state for the failure of the revival. That the state was negligent, unimaginative, authoritarian, obstructive, piecemeal, hostile and downright stupid at times, is beyond question. Even if it had been the opposite of all those things, the revival would have failed because the people in English-speaking communities did not want to revert to Irish. Forcing them to learn Irish as a second language was one thing, but the revival project wanted them to replace English with Irish as well. Why should they? English had become their language, in the same way as Irish was still the language of some Gaeltacht areas. To change the language of Kilkerrin in East Galway to Irish would have done as much violence to that community's cultural life as changing the language of Cill Chiaráin in Conamara from Irish to English.

There are examples of Irish-speaking communities within which language shift was arrested, but there are no examples of Irish being restored as the main language of any community, after language change had taken place.[41] Ráth Cairn is the only example of a geographical area becoming mainly Irish-speaking. This was of course not a case of organic change, which was hoped would happen if the revival project was to succeed. Instead it was due to it being colonised by approximately twenty-five families of Irish-speakers from the same linguistic community, who subsequently managed to hold on to Irish, in spite of official indifference for many years.[42] Using tax breaks to colonise some of the Gaeltacht areas under threat could have a stabilising effect on the linguistic balance.

We are now in a new era, the era of the Official Languages Act 2003. That it should have taken eighty years to provide a legal framework to protect the rights of Irish-speakers is a supreme example of state negligence with regard to the Irish language and raises the legitimate question as to whether a British government would have been guilty of such delay, if it was from Westminister rather than from Dáil Éireann that Ireland was governed.[43] *Is fearr go mall ná go brách*. The Official Languages Act 2003 signals an era of some hope that the tide is turning in favour of users of the language, be they within the Gaeltacht or outside the Gaeltacht. At last there is a legal mechanism in place, even though it is deliberately designed to be complicated and unwieldy.[44] It seems to place more emphasis on getting official reports and documents in translation than in getting services in Irish for Irish-speakers.

The wonder of it is that the Irish language is alive at all. Alive it is, but numbers using it as an everyday language of communication have reached the stage that any further reduction could result in a drop below the threshold necessary for survival. It is perilously close to that threshold, though there are some reasons to think that the situation can be turned around, but only if a concerted effort is made to ensure its survival. That is a realistic objective, which can mobilise support among the general public. Revival is neither realistic nor has it support, although the Irish-language movement often deludes itself into thinking that it has.

The belief that Ireland is a bilingual country is also a delusion. The only bilingual areas of Ireland are in the Gaeltacht. The danger of such delusions is that the Government will waste scarce resources and energy flogging the dead horse, while the wounded horse continues to weaken.[45] A large dose of realism, peppered with guidance from available expertise in language maintainence, would redirect the effort to one of consolidating what exists of an Irish-language community in Ireland, both inside and outside the Gaeltacht.

If we could look back in twenty years, and honestly say that language shift in the last remaining Irish-speaking strongholds has been arrested, that networks of Irish-speakers have been developed throughout the country, that audiences for Irish-language programmes without subtitles on TG4 have grown, that the number of children to whom Irish is being transmitted as a first language in the home is accelerating, than a lot will have been achieved and the survival of the language may be guaranteed.

On the other hand, if we continue to believe in the illusion that Irish can be 'revived' or 'restored' in communities where it has ceased to be used as a language of the community, then the likelihood is that Irish becomes a language of a dispersed band of well-meaning zealots, like myself, scattered around the country. It will of course continue to be used as a great national symbol of the state; will continue to be used for ornamentative and cultural reasons; will continued to be translated to satisfy the Languages Act and will continue to be studied in schools and universities just as Classical Latin and Greek were up to thirty years ago. However, that will not be enough to classify it as a living language, being transmitted organically from one generation to the next.

Future strategy needs to be driven by an ecological desire to maintain an important place for Irish in the linguistic diversity of a multicultural Ireland. This can only be done if spaces in which Irish can be used naturally are protected. That means strict planning regulations in the few remaining Irish-speaking areas which favour Irish-speaking families.

Everybody in Ireland will have suffered a loss if Irish is allowed to wither away. Those who will suffer the greatest loss are the indigenous people of the Gaeltacht, for whom Irish is more than a great national symbol. A Gaeltacht community which loses Irish breaks the continuous connection with its past and loses an enormous cultural resource. Its cultural life becomes poorer and the community becomes a target rather than an arrow in the era of the mass globilisation of culture, to paraphrase Raymond Williams.

An audit of the present position of the Irish language suggests that all is not lost and that a place can be secured for Irish in a multicultural Ireland, as the language of a minority within the country, both North and South. To secure the survival of Irish as a living language there may be a need for some official closure by the state on the revival as a national objective. If the Irish-language movement could rise to the challenge of recognising the failure of the revival effort and refocus its energies, it could reassert a leadership role once again in a national campaign to ensure the survival of Irish as a living language. Just as the republican movement has emerged as a key player in the future development of Northern Ireland by making a historical compromise in order to secure the Good Friday Agreement, the Irish-language movement could emerge from the margins and have a leading role in the development of a multicultural Ireland in which the survival of Irish would be secure.

Notes

1   Douglas Hyde, 'A Plea for the Irish Language' in Breandán Ó Conaire (ed.), *Douglas Hyde: Language, Lore and Lyrics*, Dublin, Irish Academic Press, 1986, p. 75.

2   The radical idea of revival or restoration was put forward by Eoin Mac Néill, in a paper published in *The Gaelic Journal* in March 1893, entitled 'A Plea and Plan for the Extension of the Movement to preserve and spread the Gaelic Language in Ireland', a few short months before the foundation of the Gaelic League by Mac Néill, Hyde and others.

3   It is worth noting that the decline in the number of Irish-speakers continued in Munster and Connacht during the fifteen years between 1911 and 1926, but at a slower rate, which illustrates the difficult task of halting language shift.

4   Séamas Ó hAodha was a man of many talents. He was a fine tenor and is reputed to have been the first person to sing '*Amhrán na bhFiann*' in public. He spoke French and Italian as well as Irish and English. As well as being active in the Gaelic League, he was a committed trade unionist and socialist; worked as an intelligence officer with Michael Collins and became the first secretary to Cumann na nGaedheal, on the formation of that party.

5   The article, rejected by the editor of the Gaelic League's *An Claidheamh Soluis*, was later published by Arthur Griffith in his newspaper *Sinn Féin* (February 1914).

6   '… a significant proportion of the political leaders of the State in the 1920s and 1930s subscribed to the view that "the Irish language was the most irrefutable authenticating mark of the historic Irish nation on whose behalf a national state had been demanded," and that "its restoration as the main vernacular of the people ought to be the objective of an independent state."' Gearóid Ó Tuathaigh, 'The Irish-Ireland Idea: Rationale and Relevance' in Edna Longley (ed.), *Culture in Ireland – Division or Diversity?*, Institute of Irish Studies, Queen's University Belfast, 1991, pp. 62-3.

7   The curriculum of the schools, principally the primary or "national" schools but also the secondary schools, was redefined to include the bringing about of what it was hoped would be a linguistic revolution, i.e. the displacement of English by Irish as the spoken language of the majority population. The attainment of this linguistic shift was established as a cultural imperative following independence.' Cf. Adrian Kelly, 'Cultural Imperatives: the Irish language revival and the educational system' in Joost Augusteijn (ed.), *Ireland in the 1930s*, Four Courts, Dublin, 1999, p. 29.

8   'Public Notice 4' in February 1922 stipulated that Irish be taught or used as a medium of instruction in all primary schools for not less than one hour per day. How this was to be done was not explained as less than a

third of the 22,000 lay teachers in 1922 had any qualification in Irish.

9   When Ernest Blythe directed that all forms used internally within the Department of Finance should be in Irish only, the Secretary of the Department, Joseph Brennan, pointed out that he could not have his staff signing forms they could not understand, which might be authorising the payment of large sums of money. That stopped that!

10 Brian Ó Cuív made the following assessment of the Commission's work in 1951: 'The Gaeltacht Commission … was not concerned as to whether those described as Irish-speakers did in fact use the Irish language as their normal means of expression … In spite of the illusory nature of the 1925 figures, they seem to have been accepted by the Gaeltacht commission, which accordingly made over 80 recommendations to the Government, aimed at preserving the existing *fíor-Ghaeltacht* areas and gradually extending their boundaries until they should embrace the *breac-Ghaeltacht* and finally meet one another across the intervening *Galltacht*. Even allowing that the Gaeltacht Commission was mistaken in its view as to the extent of the Gaeltacht, there was still a chance that vigorous and enlightened action would achieve some measure of success … what meagre measures were at length adopted were not adequate.' Brian Ó Cuív, *Irish Dialects and Irish-Speaking Districts*, Dublin Institute for Advanced Studies, 1951, pp. 29-30.

11 Pádraic Ó Conaire was an astute observer of human behaviour. In an article entitled 'An Dáil Nua agus an Teanga', written in July 1922, he made this observation with regard to the attitude to Irish among post-independence politicians: 'Sa tríú Dáil nuair a bheidh ceist an-chorraithe á phlé [*sic*] ag na teachtairí, is beag alt ann nach gcuirfear ina aghaidh. Ach bíodh gach duine cinnte dearfa gurb é an t-alt a bhaineann leis an teanga Ghaeilge an t-aon alt amháin nach gcuirfear ina aghaidh … Agus tá daoine ar an tríú dáil seo, agus ní hé hamháin gur cuma leo an teanga ach is fuath leo í ina gcroí istigh – cén fáth mar sin, nach gcuireann siad in aghaidh an ailt seo atá i gceist agam? An é an chaoi gur dóigh leo go mbeadh sé fánach acu? Ní hea ar chor ar bith, ach go bhfuil a fhios acu go rímhaith nach bhfuil san alt ach ornáideachas. Tá a fhios ag cairde na teanga é chomh maith le naimhde na teanga, agus fágann an dá dhream mar sin é mar scéal.' Eibhlín Ní Chionnaith, *Pádraic Ó Conaire: Scéal a Bheatha*, Cló Iar-Chonnachta, 1995, p. 188, n. 1. [In the third *Dáil* when the deputies discuss any contentious question, there are few articles which will go unchallenged. But let everyone be sure about one thing, any article regarding Irish will be the one not to go unchallenged … There are people in this third *dáil* who are not only apathetic towards Irish, they hate it in their heart of hearts – why don't they challenge the particular article in question here? Is it that they think it wouldn't be worth their while? Not at all, but they know perfectly well the article in question is

nothing more than window dressing. The enemies of the language know that as well as its friends do.]

12 In September 1934 a revised programme for primary schools increased the time to be spent at Irish, making algebra and geometry optional and removing rural science from the curriculum altogether. In 1936 Shán Ó Cuív expressed the view that the emphasis on Irish as a medium of instruction in primary schools was leading to 'a slowing of the mental development of pupils and an impaired power to express themselves or to learn.' (Adrian Kelly, *Compulsory Irish: Language and Education in Ireland 1870s-1970s*, Irish Academic Press, Dublin, 2002, p. 48.)

13 Kelly, *art. cit.*, pp. 44-5.

14 The Irish language rarely features as part – still less a central part – of the conservationist agenda; attitudes towards its predicament and future prospects I have found to be disappointingly indifferent or hostile among sections of the educated classes otherwise sensitive and enlightened in their attitudes to conservation and heritage issues. It may of course be argued – indeed it frequently is argued – that the very exclusivist claims made for Irish by some revivalists together with the shortcomings of the formulaic and bureaucratic means employed in the state language policy in the Irish state from the 1920s, produced a strong and predictable reaction, and that this accounts for the switch-off among sections of the educated and not-so-educated classes from any concern for the language.' Ó Tuathaigh, *art. cit.*, p. 67.

15 It was mandatory to achieve a pass in Irish in all state examinations and passing an Irish exam was compulsory for entry to the civil service and for promotion within the civil service.

16 The White Paper was prepared by the Government in response to the recommendations contained in the final report of *An Coimisiún um Athbheochan na Gaeilge* (1963).

17 It was not necessary to have a pass in Irish in the Leaving Certificate to matriculate with TCD, but during the 1960s Archbishop John Charles McQuaid had renewed his prohibition on Catholics in his Archdiocese from attending Trinity College.

18 Pupils sat the Group Certificate after three years of study at a Vocational School or Technical School, the only post-primary education accessible at the time to the majority of children from small farmer and working-class backgrounds, who could not afford the fees for the secondary school. A pass in the Group Certificate was necessary for entry to apprenticeships and for jobs such as clerk typist. Working-class resentment against Irish was largely based on the valid belief that it was a barrier to advancement.

19 Fergal Tobin, *The Best of Decades*, Gill and Macmillan, Dublin, 1984, pp. 152-3.

20   *ibid.*, p. 153. This solution was proposed from the platform by Dónall Ó
       Móráin and accepted by the President of LFM, Christopher Morris. The
       four speakers 'in favour of Irish' were Seán Ó hÉigeartaigh (Sáirséal agus
       Dill), the expert in modern language teaching, An tAthair Colmán Ó
       Huallacháin OFM, the Chairperson of An Coimisiún um Athbheochan
       na Gaeilge, An tAthair Tomás Ó Fiaich and the Methodist teacher and
       writer, Risteárd Ó Glaisne.

21   Addressing the inaugural meeting of the ITÉ Advisory Committee,
       Donough O'Malley had this to say: 'At present the whole position of the
       Irish language in our educational system and its place so to speak in the
       national ethos is being subjected to a great deal of critical examination. It
       is essential that all the scientific knowledge and expertise available should
       be brought to bear to find answers to the many questions being raised
       and to find solutions to the many practical problems involved in the
       revival of Irish as a spoken language among our people.'

22   Gearóid Ó Tuathaigh summarised what happened as 'a paralysis of
       political will allied to bureaucratic obstruction ...' 'Language, Literature
       and Culture in Ireland since the War' in J.J. Lee (ed.), *Ireland 1945-70*, Gill
       and Macmillan, Dublin, 1979, p. 117.

23   See Colmán Ó Huallacháin, *The Irish and Irish*, Dublin, Assisi Press, 1994,
       pp. 186-7.

24   In the 1973 election the National Coalition's manifesto on Irish included
       the following statement: 'The policy of the selective compulsion that has
       proved so disastrous for the Irish language over the past 50 years will be
       replaced by a genuine policy based on respect for and promotion of the
       Irish language and culture.'

25   Dún Chaoin school in the West Kerry Gaeltacht was officially closed by
       the Minister for Education, Pádraig Faulkner, in 1971 and the children
       were to be bussed to another Gaeltacht school in Baile an Fheirtéaraigh.
       A group of parents with support from outside the community kept the
       school open and mounted a very effective campaign of protest against the
       Government. After a week-long march from Dún Chaoin to Dublin in
       1972, the protesters were batoned off the street outside the GPO and
       some were arrested and charged. However, other Gaeltacht schools,
       which had been closed around the same time and the children sent to
       English-medium schools, remained closed when Scoil Dhún Chaoin was
       triumphantly reopened.

26   To qualify for a Higher Education Grant, it was necessary to get four
       honours grades in the Leaving Cerificate. An honours grade in Irish was
       to be counted as two for the purposes of qualifying for the grant.

27   In briefing the Cabinet on the issue, the Taoiseach Liam Cosgrave is on
       record as saying: 'It is important that the proposal should be seen as a
       positive step in favour of the language and not as a first step on the road

to its abandonment as those opposed to Irish and, equally but for different reasons, those committed to it, may be tempted to infer.' (State papers released on 1 January 2004 as reported in the *Irish Examiner* on 2 January 2004.)

28   Article 25.4.4 of *Bunreacht na hÉireann* reads as follows: 'Where the President signs the text of a Bill in one only of the official languages, an official translation shall be issued in the other official language.'

29   The leader of the Government, W.T. Cosgrave, wrote as follows to the Chairman of the newly appointed Commission, General Richard Mulcahy TD: 'We recognise also that the future of the Irish language and its part in the future of the Irish nation depend, more than anything else, on its continuing in an unbroken tradition as the language of Irish homes. This tradition is the living root from which alone organic growth is possible.'

30   The then President of Conradh na Gaeilge, Maolsheachlainn Ó Caollaí, alleged in his address to the organisation's Ard-Fheis in 1972 that children from the Gaeltacht had been put into a Mental Hospital on foot of an English language IQ test. I understand from teachers that there are still no Irish-language IQ tests suitable for testing young Gaeltacht children with little or no English. This occasionally results in Irish-speaking children being wrongly classified as mentally retarded because of low scores on English-language IQ tests.

31   The writer and actor Joe Steve Ó Neachtain expressed the views of his generation in an essay entitled 'An Pláta Fataí agus an Máilín *Tayto*' in Liam Mac Mathúna, Ciarán Mac Murchaidh and Máirín Nic Eoin (eds), *Teanga, Pobal agus Réigiún*, Coiscéim, Dublin, 2000, p. 69: 'D'imigh chuile dhuine dá raibh in aon rang liom sa scoil náisiúnta go Sasana nó go Meiriceá. Níorbh í Gaeilge na Gaeltachta an chloch ba mhó ar a bpaidrín siúd ó thug siad a n-aghaidh soir, ná níorbh í an Ghaeilge an chloch ba mhór ar mo phaidrínse ach an oiread, nuair a thosaigh mé ag obair sa gcathair a nglaoitear "Gaillimh le Gaeilge" anois uirthi. Gaillimh le drochmheas ar mo chuidse Gaeilge a bhí ann de bharr go raibh mé easpach ó thaobh an Bhéarla. Ba ghearr gur tuigeadh dom gur saoránach den dara grád mé.' [Everyone in my class in national school went to England or America. The Irish of the Gaeltacht was the least of their concerns as they headed east, and indeed it was the least of my concerns too, when I began working in that city now known as Galway of the "Gaeilge". Galway of the disregard for "Gaeilge" is what it was, since my own English was very poor. I soon understood that I was a second-class citizen.']

32   In Lindsay's autobiography he comments as follows: 'My fundamental reason for doing this was that I believe that the people of these particular areas, whether they were fíor Gaeltacht [*sic*] areas or not, had bad

housing, bad sanitation and no water.' Patrick Lindsay, *Memories*, Blackwater Press, Dublin, 1992, p. 164.

33 The revision of the Gaeltacht boundaries in 1956 suggests a process of substantial linguistic change in the more extensive eastern portion of the 1926 Gaeltacht. However a closer examination of the data would argue that most of this Breac-Gaeltacht [*sic*] area was already English-speaking in 1926. In fact, not only was the Breac-Gaeltacht [*sic*] boundary misleading, but the Gaeltacht commission appears also to have grossly over-estimated the area it regarded as Fíor-Gaeltacht [*sic*]. This was partly due to the unreliable nature of the data available to it, but it was also due to the commission's inclination to base its definition of the Gaeltacht on "potential" rather than actual patterns of language use. I would argue that patterns of language use in 1956 were very similar to those actually obtaining in 1926. The areas within which Irish was most intensively spoken in 1926 remained stable until the last two decades. Although there are now signs of progressive language shift within even the original core, at the end of the twentieth century, this area still contains communities that are largely Irish-speaking.' Pádraig Ó Riagáin, 'The Galway Gaeltacht 1926-1981: A Socio-linguistic Study of Continuity and Change' in Gerard Morgan and Raymond Gillespie (eds), *Galway – History and Society*, Geography Publications, Dublin, 1996, p. 678.

34 According to the 2002 Annual Report of Údarás na Gaeltachta there were 7,571 people working full time in Údarás-assisted employments and another 4,000 working part-time.

35 Máirtín Ó Murchú, 'Aspects of the Societal Status of Modern Irish' in Martin J. Ball (ed.), *The Celtic Languages*, Routledge, London, 1993, p. 483.

36 In the year 2002 only 4 per cent of Údarás na Gaeltachta's budget was spent on Irish-language development. This was a vast improvement from the 1 per cent devoted to the language in 1999.

37 A survey made in 1977 of twenty-four Údarás na Gaeltachta factories found that 30 per cent of management had no Irish and 16 per cent of shopfloor workers had no Irish. An Coiste Comhairleach Pleanála, *The Irish Language in a Changing Society: Shaping the Future*, Dublin, 1986, p.7.

38 J.J. Lee, *Ireland 1912-1985: Politics and Society*, Cambridge University Press, 1989, pp. 670-2.

39 In the state overall the number of 3-4 year olds using Irish on a daily basis has increased from 4,812 in 1996 to 5,991 in 2002, an increase of 24.5 per cent. A 5 per cent increase was recorded for the Gaeltacht in the same period for pre-school children.

40 This figure is based on studies I have done on actual use of Irish in Gaeltacht areas, as revealed by data from Census 1996 and on data from the Department of the Gaeltacht with regard to Scéim Labhairt na

Gaeilge, published in *Cuisle* (February 1999) and in *Foinse* (5 January, 2003).

41   Desmond Fennell observed in 1969 that 'not a single street, not a single pub or shop or café in Galway – not to mention Dublin or in any other city – has become *even predominantly* Irish-speaking during the past 50 years.' ('Language Revival: is it already a lost cause?', *The Irish Times*, 21 January 1969)

42   The Ráth Cairn colony was established in 1935, but the Government refused the give it full Gaeltacht recognition 'because it is not considered necessary that all the Gaeltacht schemes, which have their origin in the circumstances of extreme congestion in the West, should be extended to parts of County Meath.' (Government White Paper on the Restoration of the Irish Language, 1965). Recognition eventually was granted in 1967 after a persistent campaign.

43   It is worth noting that the then Minister for Welsh Affairs, Sir Keith Joseph, set up a Committee to examine the 'Legal Status of the Welsh Language' as far back as 1963 and the first Welsh Language Act was passed by Westminister in 1967. A second Welsh Language Act, on which the recent Official Languages Act was modelled to a large extent, was passed in 1993. Another example of a better official deal for Welsh from Westminister is the setting up of the Welsh language TV Channel in 1982, while the Irish language had to wait until 1996.

44   The Bill was signed into law in July 2003. At the time of writing, February 2004, the first stage in the preparation of a draft scheme for any public body under the Act has not yet been completed. There are eight different stages to the mechanism for agreeing a 'scheme' between a public body and the Minister for the Gaeltacht, before the compliance with the scheme comes within the remit of the Official Languages Commissioner.

45   A press release in January 2003, announcing the intention of the Minister for Gaeltacht, Éamon Ó Cuív, to set up a review of the Gaeltacht boundaries, went on to say that there would be an emphasis on weaker Gaeltacht areas in language planning in the Gaeltacht. This could be just soothing words for the party faithful in those areas or it could be that the Minister is foolish enough to believe that Irish can be revived in Uíbh Ráthach, Acaill, Bearna, Maigh Cuilinn and Baile Chláir na Gaillimhe, places where Irish has ceased to be used for more than a generation by any significant number of people.